Y0-ABH-219

Light & Delicious

Presented By
**Home Economics Teachers of
California, Nevada and Arizona**

Editor
Gerry Murry Henderson

Graphic Design, Typography and Production
Mike Burk Production Services, Long Beach, CA

**Library of Congress Catalog
Card No. 83-072750
ISBN 0-914159-12-7**

Light & Delicious

We owe special credit and thanks to all who
contributed towards publishing this year's book:

Home Economics Teachers of California, Nevada and Arizona,
who contributed all these "Light & Delicious" recipes! **Gerry
Murry Henderson,** of Temple City High School, who carefully
edits all the recipes. **Nancy Freeman,** our CCC Office Manager,
who literally "Runs the Business"! **Mike Burk,** for all graphic
design, page layouts and production. **Jeremy Bernstein,** of KNI,
Inc., in Anaheim, for quality printing and binding. **Doug
Herrema,** our "Directeur" of Publications, titles and photography.
Doug Pierce, who drives farther, sees more schools and sells
more books than any of us! **Russ Herrema, Bill Horton, Bill
O'Brien** and **"Rich" Richardson,** who deliver and pick-up books
all over California, Nevada and Arizona (better than the pony
express!).

Special thanks to the following food companies and councils for
donating our color photography: **American Sheep Industry,**
Englewood, Colorado; **California Apricot Advisory Board,**
Walnut Creek, California; **California Strawberry Advisory
Board,** Watsonville, California; **Dole Food Company,** San
Francisco, California; **Hershey Foods Corporation,** Hershey,
Pennsylvania; **National Fisheries Institute,** Arlington, Virginia;
National Livestock and Meat Board, Chicago, Illinois; **National
Pork Producers,** Des Moines, Iowa; **U.S.A. Rice Council,**
Houston, Texas; **Wisconsin Milk Marketing Board,** Madison,
Wisconsin. Interior Art from **Art Parts** by Ron and Joe.

And certainly, ***thanks to all the purchasers of this book,*** as
it supports local schools and children, and creates many jobs for
others!

Sincerely,

Grady W. Reed

Grady W. Reed, Owner
California Cookbook Company

P.S. Please note the reorder form on page 160.

Table of Contents

On Our Front Cover:
Fruit Salad with Strawberries and Cream, page 35
Apricot Mixed Grill, page 80
Grecian Lamb Kabobs, page 69
Chocolate Angel Cake, page 132

Home Economics Teachers
Advisory Committee

We would like to thank the following special people for their advice, ideas and support over the years…

Phyllis Arkus
Lakewood High School, Lakewood

Mary Carr
Enterprise High School, Redding

Carole Delap
Golden West High School, Visalia

Pam Fecchino
Cimmaron-Memorial High School
Las Vegas, Nevada

Pam Ford
Temecula Valley High School, Temecula

Donna Geer, Assistant Principal
Chino High School, Chino

Renee Glennan
Sequoia Jr. High School, Simi Valley

Donna Hamilton
Del Oro High School, Loomis

Gerry Henderson
Temple City High School, Temple City

Gage Hewes
So. Pasadena High School, So. Pasadena

Grace Hibma
Office of L.A. County Superintendent of
Schools, Consultant Consumer &
Homemaking Education

Donna Hulen
Los Alamitos High School, Los Alamitos

Dottie Jones
Etiwanda High School, Etiwanda

Mary Lash
Paramount High School, Paramount

Helen Lievre
La Cañada High School, La Cañada

Karen Lopez
San Luis Obispo High School,
San Luis Obispo

Jeri Lundy
Grossmont High School, La Mesa

Darlene Lupul
Tokay High School, Lodi

Dale Matsuno
Bell Gardens High School, Bell Gardens

Doris Oitzman
Victor Valley High School, Victorville

Linda Paskins
Cordova High School, Rancho Cordova

Susie Pendleton
Cerritos High School, Cerritos

Roberta Priestley
Alhambra High School, Alhambra

Mary Rector
Valley High School, Las Vegas, Nevada

Lynda Ruth
La Mirada High School, La Mirada

Dianne Sheats
Gridley High School, Gridley

Bonnie Shrock
Kearny High School, San Diego

Jill Sweet-Gregory
Santa Paula High School, Santa Paula

Marianne Traw
Ball Junior High School, Anaheim

Betty Wells
Oroville High School, Oroville

Kathryn P. Whitten
Regional Supervisor Home Economics
Education, Fresno

Healthy Cooking & Eating Tips

Enjoy Eating!

The food we eat depends on our history, culture and environment. What we eat and how much also depends on our energy and nutrient needs.

Our diet is important, especially when we're young

Healthful diets help our children develop, grow, and do their best in school. The food choices we make can also help to reduce our risks for diseases such as diabetes, heart disease, osteoporosis, stroke and certain cancers. The leading causes of death and disability among Americans.

A good diet can reduce major risk factors for chronic diseases–factors such as obesity, high cholesterol, and high blood pressure.

Exercise helps you with a healthful diet

How much you need to eat varies by age and activity level. Older adults typically need less food than their younger, more active counterparts. This is mainly due to older adults decreased activity.

Nearly all Americans need to be more active. Most Americans spend much of their working day in activities that requires little energy. In addition, many Americans of all ages now spend a lot of leisure time each day being inactive, for example, watching television or working at a computer. A sedentary lifestyle is unhealthful. Increasing the calories spent in daily activities helps to maintain health, and allows people to eat a nutritious and enjoyable diet.

Good food choices mean good health

Research has shown that certain diets raise risks for chronic diseases. Such diets are high in fat, saturated fat, cholesterol, and salt. They contain more calories than your body needs. They are also low in grain products, vegetables, fruit and fiber.

Eating patterns are important

Our pattern of eating is important too. Snacks provide daily calories for many Americans. Unless nutritious snacks are part of the daily meal plan, **snacking may lead to weight gain.**

Sound Advice

Try to maintain your body weight by balancing what you eat with how active you are. If you tend to be sedentary, **become more active.** If you are already active, **continue** the same level of activity as you age. More activity is better than less, and any is better than none.

Reduce Fat in Cooking

Use fats and oils sparingly.

Use the Nutrition Facts Label to help you choose foods lower in fat, saturated fat and cholesterol.

Eat plenty of grain products, vegetables and fruits

Choose low fat milk products, lean meats, fish, poultry, beans and peas to get essential nutrients without substantially increasing calorie and saturated fat

Trim visible fat from meat and remove skin from poultry.

Use non-stick sprays to coat pans.

Brown meats by broiling rather than sauteing in fat.

Use water-packed canned fish

Use water-packed canned chicken

Use poultry, fish and veal in place of red meats when appropriate.

Prepare vegetables with herbs and spices rather than adding fat or cream.

In recipes for many baked products, the sugar can be reduced ⅓ to ¼ without harming the final product.

Use Substitutes

Instead of...	Try using
Butter	Low-calorie margarine
Heavy cream	Evaporated skim milk
Mayonnaise	Low-calorie mayonnaise
Whole Milk	Skim or low-fat milk
Sour cream	Plain low-fat yogurt
Cheeses	Skim milk cheeses or low-fat cottage cheese
Whole eggs	Egg whites or egg substitutes.

Food Group Pyramid

Foods contain combinations of nutrients and other healthful substances. No single food can supply all nutrients in the amounts you need. To make sure you get all of the nutrients and other substances needed for health, choose the recommended number of daily servings from each of the **five major food groups** displayed below.

The pyramid illustrates the importance of balance among food groups in a daily eating pattern. Most of the daily servings of food should be selected from the food groups that are the largest in the picture and closest to the base of the pyramid.

Choose most of your foods from the grain products group, the vegetable group and the fruit group. Eat moderate amounts of foods from the milk group, the meat and beans group. Choose sparingly foods that provide few nutrients and are high in fat and sugars.

Fats, Oils and Sweets Group
Use Sparingly

Milk, Yogurt and Cheese Group
2 - 3 Servings

Meat, Poultry, Fish, Beans, Eggs and Nuts Group
2 - 3 Servings

Vegetable Group
3 - 5 Servings

Fruit Group
2 - 4 Servings

Bread, Cereal, Rice and Pasta Group
6 - 11 Servings

Serving Sizes

These servings are based on the Food Group Pyramid on page 6.

Grain Group

- 1 slice of bread
- 1 ounce of ready-to-eat cereal
- ½ cup of cooked cereal, rice or pasta

Vegetable Group

- 1 cup of raw leafy vegetables
- ½ cup of other vegetables cooked or chopped raw
- ¾ cup of vegetable juice

Fruit Group

- 1 medium apple, banana or orange
- ½ cup chopped, cooked or canned fruit
- ¾ cup of fruit juice

Milk Group

- 1 cup of milk or yogurt
- 1 ½ ounces of natural cheese
- 2 ounces of processed cheese

Meat and Beans Group

- 2-3 ounces of cooked lean meat, poultry or fish
- ½ cup of cooked dry beans or 1 egg counts as 1 ounce of lean meat.
- 2 tablespoons of peanut butter or ⅓ cup of nuts count as 1 ounce of meat.

The Fast Food Lane

Here are some tips to use when choosing and ordering at fast food establishments:

Choose a small roast beef or a small hamburger

Try to stay away from burgers with names like "Whopper", "Super", "Jumbo", "Double" or "Triple". The extra meat and the special sauce give you two or three

Healthy Cooking & Eating Tips
times the calories and fat.

Pass up the creamy sauces

Mayonnaise and tartar sauce add over 100 calories of fat to each sandwich.

Go for broiled or baked fish or chicken

They contain substantially less fat and calories than their deep-fried counterparts. Don't be fooled... the deep-fried fish and chicken sandwiches served in most fast food restaurants contain as much or more fat and calories as the hamburgers.

Skip the "Extra Crispy"

The coating adds much more fat to chicken and fish.

Order your baked potato plain

Or with just vegetables. All the other toppings add extra fat. Sour cream or cottage cheese toppings are a slightly better choice than butter, margarine or grated cheese.

Use low-calorie dressings

Use cottage cheese or vinegar with just a little oil to top your salad from the salad bar or a showcase.

Order just the basics

Order simple at the drive-up window. Serve them at home with low (or non)-fat milk, vegetables and fruit.

Make your own fast food meals

Select convenient, single-serving cans or boxes of fruit and vegetable juice, lowfat yogurt, lowfat pre-sliced meats (at least 95% fat-free), whole grain bread, whole fruits, raw vegetables, small boxes of raisins, etc. You can build a lowfat, nutritious meal for probably less than it costs for a meal from a fast food place.

Are You Overweight?

Many Americans gain weight in adulthood, increasing their risk for high blood pressure, heart disease, stroke, diabetes, certain types of cancer, arthritis, breathing problems and other illnesses.

Evaluate your body weight

Healthy weight ranges for adult men and women of all ages are shown in the chart below. **See where your weight falls on the chart for people of your height.** The health risks due to excess weight appear to be the same for older as for younger adults. Weight ranges are shown in the

If you need to lose weight

You do not need to lose weight if your weight is already within the healthy range in the chart. If you have gained less than 10 pounds since you reached your adult height, and if you are otherwise healthy.

If you are overweight and have excess abdominal fat, a weight-related medical problem, or a family history of such problems, **you need to lose weight.** Healthy diets and exercise can help people maintain a healthy weight, and may also help them lose weight. It is important to recognize that being overweight is a chronic condition which can only be controlled with long-term

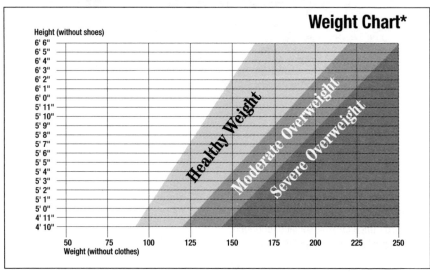

chart because people of the same weight may have equal amounts of body fat but different amounts of muscle and bone. The ranges do not mean that it is healthy to gain weight, even within the same weight range.

The further you are above the healthy weight range for your height, the higher your weight-related risk. Weights slightly below the range may be healthy for some people but are sometimes the result of health problems, especially when weight loss is unintentional.

changes. To reduce caloric intake, **eat less fat** and **control portion sizes.**

If you are not physically active, spend less time in sedentary activities such as watching television, and be more active throughout the day. As people lose weight, the body becomes more efficient at using energy and the rate of weight loss may decrease. Increased physical activity will help you to continue losing weight and to avoid gaining it back.

*Source: Report of the Dietary Guidelines Advisory Committee on the Dietary Guidelines for Americans, 1995, pages 23-24.

Appetizers & Beverages

Alicia's Spinach Dip

Serves 8   *341 calories, 1 fat gram*

10 ounces frozen spinach, chopped
1 package dry vegetable soup mix
16 ounces nonfat plain yogurt
$1/2$ cup nonfat mayonnaise
3 green onions, finely chopped
8 ounces water chestnuts, chopped (optional)
dash tabasco sauce
round loaf sourdough bread, unsliced

Thaw and squeeze all moisture from spinach. In a bowl, mix together soup mix, yogurt and mayonnaise until well blended. Stir in spinach, green onions and water chestnuts. Add tabasco to taste. Cover and chill for 2 hours. Before serving, hollow out round sourdough loaf. Stir dip and place inside hollowed out bread. Serve with bread pieces for dipping.

"Always a favorite at any gathering."
Alicia Pucci   **Kenilworth Junior High School, Petaluma, CA**

Artichoke Parmesan Spread

Makes 3 1/4 cups   *64 calories, 1 fat gram*

1 cup fat free mayonnaise
$1/2$ cup Parmesan cheese, freshly grated
1 cup soft bread crumbs
$1/4$ teaspoon reduced sodium worcestershire sauce
$1/4$ teaspoon hot sauce
$1/8$ teaspoon garlic powder
2 (14 ounce) cans artichoke hearts, drained and chopped
nonstick cooking spray

Combine first 6 ingredients, gently fold in artichokes. Spoon into 1 quart casserole coated with nonstick cooking spray. Cover and bake at 350 degrees for 20 minutes, or until thoroughly heated. Serve with assorted raw vegetables or lowfat crackers. To cook in microwave, follow same directions, only cover with waxed paper and microwave at medium power 12 to 14 minutes, stirring twice during cooking.

"A healthier version of an old favorite."
Nancy Schoner   **Kraemer Middle School, Placentia, CA**

Bea's Pickled Mushrooms

Serves 10   *125 calories, 11 fat grams*

2 pounds fresh button mushrooms
1 cup cider vinegar
$1/2$ cup salad oil
1 clove garlic, halved
$1/2$ teaspoon salt
$1/2$ teaspoon white or black pepper
$1/2$ teaspoon dried thyme
$1/2$ tablespoon dried oregano
$1/2$ tablespoon chervil
1 bay leaf
parsley, chopped

Wash mushrooms thoroughly. Blanch mushrooms by dropping into boiling water for a 10 - 15 seconds; remove immediately and rinse under cool water; drain. Combine all ingredients and place in a jar. Allow to marinate for at least a week before serving.

"Bea comes up with the greatest recipes. You won't be able to eat just one. Thanks for sharing, Bea!"
Penny Childers   **Ramona High School, Ramona, CA**

Berry Banana Breakfast Shake

Serves 2   *186 calories, 1 fat gram*

    2 extra-ripe, medium Dole bananas, peeled
    $3/4$ cup Dole Country Raspberry Juice
    $3/4$ cup lowfat buttermilk
    $1/2$ teaspoon vanilla
    2 ice cubes

Cut bananas in thirds; add to blender with remaining ingredients. Whir until smooth. Serve.
Dole Food Company

Black Bean Tortilla Pinwheels

Serves 16   *159 calories, 6 fat grams*

    1 (8 ounce) package lite cream cheese, softened
    1 cup lite dairy sour cream
    1 cup Wisconsin Monterey Jack cheese, shredded
    $1/4$ cup pimento-stuffed green olives, well drained, chopped
    $1/4$ cup red onion, chopped
    $1/2$ teaspoon seasoned salt
    $1/8$ teaspoon garlic powder
    1 (15 ounce) can black beans, drained
    5 (10 inch) flour tortillas
    salsa

Combine cream cheese and sour cream; mix until well blended. Stir in Monterey Jack cheese, olives, onions and seasonings. Chill 2 hours. Puree beans in food processor or blender. Spread each tortilla with thin layer of beans. Spread cream cheese mixture over beans. Roll up tightly. Chill. Cut into 3/4" slices. Serve with salsa.
Wisconsin Milk Marketing Board

Cocktail Party Meatballs

Serves 32   *28 calories, 1 fat gram*

    nonstick cooking spray
    $1/4$ cup nonfat cottage cheese
    2 egg whites
    2 teaspoons worcestershire sauce
    $1/2$ cup + 2 tablespoons dry plain bread crumbs
    8 ounces ground turkey breast
    6 ounces turkey sausage, casings removed
    2 tablespoons onion, minced
    2 tablespoons green pepper, minced
    $1/2$ cup fresh parsley, snipped
    $1/4$ cup celery leaves, minced

Spray a cookie sheet with nonstick cooking spray and set aside. In a large bowl, stir together cottage cheese, egg whites, worcestershire sauce and 1/2 cup bread crumbs. Stir in ground turkey breast, turkey sausage, onion and green pepper. Shape into 32 meatballs. On sheet of waxed paper, combine parsley, celery leaves and remaining bread crumbs. Roll meatballs in parsley mixture until evenly coated. Preheat broiler. Transfer meatballs to prepared cookie sheet. Broil 3" to 4" from heat source for 10 to 12 minutes, turning occasionally, until browned on all sides and no longer pink in center. Serve with cocktail toothpicks.

Phyllis Arkus   Lakewood High School, Lakewood, CA

Delicious Deviled Eggs

Serves 8   *89 calories, 5 fat grams*

8 eggs, hard cooked, cooled
1/2 cup lowfat cottage cheese
2 teaspoons vinegar
1 1/2 teaspoon mustard
1/2 teaspoon salt
1/4 teaspoon pepper

Halve the eggs lengthwise, remove yolks. Combine egg yolks with remaining ingredients and blend until smooth. Spoon mixture into egg halves and garnish as desired.

"An easy, low-fat appetizer that everyone will enjoy!"
Linda Woolley   La Sierra High School, Riverside, CA

Fake & Easy Cappuccino

Serves 1   *110 calories, 0 fat grams*

6 ounces boiling water
2 to 4 teaspoonfuls of your favorite instant coffee beverage
6 ounces nonfat milk
sugar, if desired
dash cinnamon

Add boiling water to instant coffee beverage (doubling the amount you would normally use for a regular cup of coffee). Steam nonfat milk in microwave until hot, approximately 60 seconds. Combine milk with coffee, adding sugar to taste and top with dash of cinnamon.

"This recipe was donated by my mom, Patricia Franco. It even gets frothy on the top like regular cappuccino, and takes no time at all for a nice warm, different kind of coffee taste."
Amy Bean   Cabrillo High School, Lompoc, CA

Fantastic Slush

Serves 6 - 12   *217 calories, .3 fat grams*

1 (6 ounce) frozen orange juice concentrate
1 (6 ounce) frozen lemonade concentrate
1 large can pineapple juice
1 1/2 cups sugar
6 cups hot water
5 bananas, mashed
2 cups diet lemon-lime soda

Mix orange juice concentrate, lemonade concentrate and pineapple juice together. Dissolve sugar in hot water. Add bananas and dissolved sugar to juice mixture; mix thoroughly. Place 2 cup portions of slush in ziploc bags and freeze. To serve: mix 2 cups slush with 2 cups diet lemon-lime soda in blender at high speed. Serve immediately.

"Jan Stocking, from the city of Orange, gave me this delicious recipe. You may substitute Slice, 7-Up, or ginger ale for the lemon lime soda."
Bonnie Landin   **Garden Grove High School, Garden Grove, CA**

Fat Free Cream Cheese Salsa Spread

Serves 8   *126 calories, 5.5 fat grams*

8 ounces fat free cream cheese
16 ounces salsa
2 tablespoons cilantro, chopped (optional)

Place brick of cream cheese on a plate with a rim; let stand 30 minutes to soften. Pour half of the salsa over and around cream cheese. Sprinkle with chopped cilantro, if desired. Add remaining salsa as needed. Serve with fat free, baked chips.
Roberta Priestley   **Alhambra High School, Alhambra, CA**

Festive Spinach Dip

Serves 12   *36 calories, 0 fat grams*

10 ounces frozen chopped spinach, thawed and drained
1 cup plain nonfat yogurt
1/3 cup reduced calorie margarine
1/4 cup onion, chopped
2 tablespoons parsley flakes
1/2 teaspoon pepper
1/2 teaspoon rosemary leaves

Chop spinach finely. Mix all ingredients together; cover and chill. Serve with whole wheat crackers or crisp vegetable sticks.
Margaret Wolfe   **Linden High School, Linden, CA**

Fruity Smoothie

Serves 2 - 3   *350 calories, .5 fat grams*

1 cup juice (your choice)
1 cup nonfat fruit flavored yogurt
1 cup frozen berries
4 ice cubes
sugar, to taste

Combine all ingredients in blender and mix well.

"This is a great breakfast or snack. Experiment with different juices, yogurts and fruits. Iced tea even works!"
Beth Leighton   **Helix High School, La Mesa, CA**

Hummus Dip

Serves 8   *580 calories, 12 fat grams*

2 cloves garlic
2 lemons, juiced
1 (6 ounce) can chickpeas
pinch of salt
2 tablespoons olive oil
pinch of paprika

Peel and chop garlic and squeeze juice from lemons. Put everything except paprika in blender and blend until smooth. Add a little water if needed. Pour on to a serving dish and sprinkle with paprika. Serve as a dip with pita pockets.

"My 2 year old son's favorite thing - he loves to dip the bread!"
Kathleen Yonter   **Burkholder Middle School, Henderson, NV**

Mexican Peppered Wings

Makes 20   *252 calories, 17 fat grams*

4 pounds chicken wings, cut at joint
1 teaspoon salt
$1/2$ to 1 teaspoon ground red pepper
$1/3$ cup lime juice
1 to 2 jalapeno peppers, seeded and minced
1 clove garlic, minced
2 tablespoons fresh cilantro, chopped (or 1 teaspoon dried)
$1/2$ teaspoon red pepper flakes

Preheat broiler or prepare grill. Place wings on broiler pan or directly onto grill. Sprinkle with salt and ground red pepper. Broil or grill 15 minutes, turning until wings are browned. Meanwhile, in a bowl, combine remaining ingredients. Add wings, toss to coat. Serve with Ranch or Blue Cheese dressing, if desired.
Coleen LeMay   **Brea-Olinda High School, Brea, CA**

Nutty Chicken Fingers

Serves 5   *217 calories, 10 fat grams*

1/3 cup cornflake crumbs
1/2 cup pecans, finely chopped
1 tablespoon dried parsley flakes
1/8 teaspoon salt
1/8 teaspoon garlic powder
12 ounces boneless, skinless chicken breast halves, cut into 1" strips
2 tablespoons nonfat milk

In a shallow dish, combine cornflake crumbs, pecans, parsley, salt and garlic powder. Dip chicken in milk, then roll in crumb mixture. Bake at 400 degrees in a 15" x 10" x 1" baking pan for 7 to 9 minutes or until chicken is tender and no longer pink.

"Serve with fat free Ranch style dressing for a lowfat taste treat compared to the usual deep fried chicken nuggets. My students love them."
Sue Hope   Lompoc High School, Lompoc, CA

Pretzel Nachos

Serves 4   *182 calories, 0 fat grams*

4 cups Fat Free Pretzels
4 slices sharp cheddar cheese, fat free
1 cup salsa
1/2 cup fat free sour cream

Place pretzels twists on a microwave safe platter. Top with strips of cheese. Microwave on medium powder about 1 minute or until cheese melts. Top with salsa and sour cream.

"Great fat free appetizer or between meal snack."
Janet Giron   Montclair High School, Montclair, CA

Refreshing Fruit Spritzer

Serves 8   *74 calories, .1 fat grams*

1 cup boiling water
6 bags orange herb tea
1 (6 ounce) can frozen lemonade concentrate, thawed
2 cups apricot nectar
4 cups lime-flavored sparkling mineral water, chilled
lemon slices, optional

Pour boiling water over tea bags; cover and steep for 5 minutes. Discard tea bags. Stir in lemonade concentrate and nectar. Chill thoroughly. Stir in mineral water just before serving. Serve over ice. Garnish with lemon slices.

"On one of our summer trips to the Hawaiian Islands, my daughter had this spritzer on a field trip to the North Shore of Oahu!"
Elizabeth Ward   Raney Intermediate School, Corona, CA **15**

Spicy Tuna Dip

Serves 12   *55 calories, 0 fat grams*

1 (12 ounce) can tuna fish, packed in water
1 (8 ounce) bottle chili sauce
3 tablespoons lemon juice
dash tabasco sauce
large bag baked corn chips

Drain tuna; mix with chili sauce and lemon juice. Add tabasco sauce, to taste. Chill and serve with corn chips.

Gage Hewes   South Pasadena High School, So. Pasadena, CA

Tex Mex Black Bean Dip

Serves 12   *276 calories, 2 fat grams*

2 (15 ounce) cans black beans, drained
1 teaspoon oil
1 cup onion, chopped
4 cloves garlic, minced
1 cup tomato, chopped
$2/3$ cup salsa
1 teaspoon ground cumin
1 teaspoon chili powder
$1/2$ cup reduced fat Monterey jack cheese, shredded
$1/2$ cup cilantro, chopped
2 tablespoons fresh lime juice

Place black beans in a bowl, partially mash until chunky; set aside. Heat oil in nonstick skillet. Add onion and garlic. Saute 4 minutes or until tender. Add beans, tomatoes, salsa, ground cumin and chili powder. Cook 5 minutes, until thickened, stirring constantly. Remove from heat. Add cheese and remaining ingredients, stirring until cheese melts. Serve warm or at room temperature.

"Serve this with reduced fat tortilla chips."
Louise Sears-Miller   Swainston Middle School, N. Las Vegas, NV

Yummy Salsa

Serves 8   *23 calories, 0 fat grams*

1 can Mexican-style stewed tomatoes
$1/4$ to $1/2$ can green chiles or jalapenos, diced
2 stalks green onions, finely chopped
2 to 4 tablespoons cilantro or parsley
dash salt
pepper, to taste
cumin, to taste
chili powder, to taste

garlic powder, to taste
1 tomato, chopped

Combine stewed tomatoes, chilies, green onion, cilantro and spices in blender and blend 5 to 10 seconds, or to desired chunkiness. Add chopped tomato just before serving.

"Use this as dip with carrot and celery sticks, and you have as close to zero calories as you can get!"
Kathy Sandoz   **Mesa Junior High School, Mesa, AZ**

Yvonne's Spinach Dip

Serves 10   *45 calories, 1 fat gram*

2 cups lowfat cottage cheese
1 (10 ounce) package frozen spinach, chopped, thawed and drained
1/2 (1.25 ounce) envelope dry onion soup mix
2 tablespoons lowfat mayonnaise
1 clove garlic, minced
1 to 2 drops hot pepper sauce (optional)
assorted fresh vegetables or whole wheat pita bread, cut into wedges

In a food processor container fitted with steel blade, combine cottage cheese, spinach, dry onion soup mix, mayonnaise, garlic and hot pepper sauce. Process until smooth, stopping to scrape down sides. Chill before serving. Serve with vegetables or pita bread wedges.

"Borrowed so long ago, I don't remember the source, but it's always popular at get togethers."
Yvonne M. Jones   **Ceres High School, Ceres, CA**

Soups

Black Bean Soup

Serves 8   ***290 calories, 5 fat grams***

- 1/4 cup olive oil
- 1/4 pound lean, cooked ham, cut into pieces
- 1/4 pound turkey bacon, diced
- 1 large onion, diced
- 4 cloves garlic, minced or pressed
- 3 stalks celery, chopped
- 1 pound dried black beans, cooked
- 1/2 teaspoon cayenne pepper
- 2 teaspoons ground cumin
- 2 cans chicken broth
- 2 cups water
- 1/2 cup dry sherry
- 1/4 cup wine vinegar

Heat oil in large quart pan over medium-high heat. Add ham, bacon, onion, garlic and celery. Cook until bacon is done and onions are soft, about 5 to 7 minutes; drain off excess fat. Add beans, cayenne pepper, cumin, chicken broth and water. Bring to a boil over high heat; reduce heat, cover and simmer until beans mash easily, 1 1/2 to 2 hours. In food processor or blender, blend soup, a portion at a time, until smooth. Return to pan and heat, adding sherry and vinegar. If too thick, add water.

"Serve with warm French bread, tortillas and sour cream. This is a great recipe if you like black beans. Serve up and enjoy!"
Marshawn Porter   **Arroyo Grande High School, Arroyo Grande, CA**

Cabbage Soup

Serves 8   *238 calories, 10 fat grams*

- 2 (46 ounce) cans tomato juice
- 1 green pepper, diced
- 2 tablespoons onion flakes
- 1/4 cup lemon juice
- 6 teaspoons instant bouillon, chicken or beef
- 2 cloves garlic, minced
- 3 pounds cabbage, shredded
- 1 pound extra lean ground beef, cooked and well drained
- salt and pepper, to taste

In large Dutch oven, combine all ingredients and simmer for 1 hour.

"Great warmed up the next day."
Ida Alvey   Eldorado High School, Las Vegas, NV

Chicken Vegetable Soup

Serves 6   *275 calories, 6 fat grams*

- 1 whole chicken
- 1 onion, chopped
- 8 cups water
- 1 cup onion, finely chopped
- 1 cup carrots, sliced
- 1 cup celery, sliced
- 1/2 cup mushrooms, sliced
- 1 cup corn, frozen
- 1 cup dry noodles

Cut chicken into pieces; remove skin. Place in large kettle with 1 chopped onion and water. Simmer for 2 to 3 hours. Remove chicken pieces and debone. Strain broth into bowl and freeze overnight. Next day, remove fat from top of broth. Return broth to kettle and add remaining onion, carrots, celery, mushrooms, corn and noodles, simmering until cooked, about 20 to 30 minutes.

"This is very filling and delicious."
Barbara A. Ford   Cope Middle School, Redlands, CA

Delicious Turkey or Chicken Noodle Soup

Serves 30   *198 calories, 5 fat grams*

1 turkey or 4 chickens, roasted, boned and skinned
3 onions, diced
8 carrots, diced
8 stalks celery, diced
9 cloves garlic, minced
1 teaspoon dried parsley
4 teaspoons salt
6 teaspoons chicken bouillon granules
1 bay leaf
4 cups small egg noodles

After roasting turkey or chickens, pick off all remaining meat and place in freezer for later use in soup. In an 8 quart or larger pot, cover bones with water. Bring to a boil. Add 1 diced onion, 1 diced carrot, 1 diced celery stalk, 2 smashed cloves garlic, parsley, 2 teaspoons salt, chicken bouillon granules and bay leaf. Reduce heat; simmer, covered 3 hours. Strain broth, discarding all solid ingredients. Chill over night. Next day, scrape fat from top surface (stock will have jelled). Bring stock to a boil. Add remaining vegetables and salt. In another pot, cook egg noodles according to package directions; drain and add to soup. Adjust seasonings. Add reserved turkey or chicken meat and heat through. Refrigerate soup again overnight as soup seems to get better over time. If you can't wait - enjoy! Bring to a slow boil before serving next day.

"Inexpensive, lowfat, good for you and promises to warm your soul and soften many of life's problems."
Carol Goddard   **Alhambra High School, Alhambra, CA**

Fat Burning Soup

Serves 8   *92 calories, 1 fat gram*

5 bunches green onions, chopped
2 (28 ounce) cans tomatoes
1 large head cabbage, shredded
2 green peppers, chopped
1 bunch celery, chopped
1 package Lipton onion soup mix
Seasonings: add to taste (optional)
salt, pepper, curry powder, parsley, bouillon, hot sauce

In large pot, combine all ingredients and add just enough water to cover. Bring to a boil and boil for 10 minutes; lower heat to simmer, cover and continue cooking until vegetables are tender, about 20 minutes.

"It actually works to help you lose weight!"
Brenda Burke   **Mt. Whitney High School, Visalia, CA**

Garden Tomato Soup

Serves 4   *127 calories, 2 fat grams*

4 large tomatoes, peeled and coarsely chopped
1 cup chicken broth, fat removed
4 green onions, sliced
1 small cucumber, peeled and sliced
$^1/_2$ cup green pepper, diced
1 cup tomato juice
juice of 1 lemon
2 teaspoons sugar
1 tablespoon salt
$^1/_4$ teaspoon seasoned pepper

Combine tomatoes, broth, onion, cucumber and green pepper in saucepan. Bring to a boil and simmer, covered, 5 minutes. Add remaining ingredients; cover and simmer another 10 minutes. Chill. Serve cold.

"This soup is very refreshing in the summer."
Kathy Arthur   **La Sierra High School, Riverside, CA**

Gram's Vegetable Soup

Serves 8   *110 calories, 1 fat gram*

1 quart tomato juice
2 cans chicken broth, fat skimmed
1(12 ounce) package frozen vegetables
1 (8 ounce) package frozen potatoes, cubed
1 $^1/_2$ teaspoons oregano
1 $^1/_2$ teaspoons garlic salt
1 $^1/_2$ teaspoons thyme
1 $^1/_2$ teaspoons basil
$^1/_2$ head cabbage, sliced
dash salt and pepper

Pour tomato juice and chicken broth into large pot. Add frozen vegetables and potatoes. Stir in seasonings; bring to boil then reduce heat and simmer 5 minutes. Turn off heat. Slice cabbage into pot and serve. Season with salt and pepper to taste.

"My 92-year young grandmother has been serving this soul warming broth to my 97-year young grandfather for the better part of their 73-year marriage."
Julie Carriere   **North Monterey County High School, Castroville, CA**

Hearty Chicken and Rice Soup

Serves 8   *184 calories, 4 fat grams*

10 cups chicken broth
1 medium onion, chopped
1 cup celery, sliced
1 cup carrots, sliced
1/4 cup fresh parsley, chopped
1/2 teaspoon cracked black pepper
1/2 teaspoon dried thyme leaves
1 bay leaf
1 1/2 cups chicken, cubed (about 3/4 pound)
2 cups rice, cooked
2 tablespoons lime juice
lime slices, for garnish

Combine broth, onion, celery, carrots, parsley, pepper, thyme and bay leaf in Dutch oven. Bring to a boil; stir once or twice. Reduce heat; simmer, uncovered, 10 to 5 minutes. Add chicken; simmer, uncovered, 5 to 10 minutes or until chicken is cooked. Remove and discard bay leaf. Stir in rice and lime juice just before serving. Garnish with lime slices.

USA Rice Council

Hearty Lentil Soup

Serves 4   *260 calories, 3 fat grams*

1 cup dry lentils
1 cup carrots, sliced
1/2 cup onion, chopped
2 teaspoons salt free seasoning, such as Mrs. Dash
3 cups water
1 cup ham, cooked and diced
1 (16 ounce) can tomatoes, cut up

Combine all ingredients in a large saucepan and simmer for 1 1/2 hours.

"It's so easy and so delicious for a warming, winter meal."
Val Herford   **Mesa Intermediate School, Palmdale, CA**

Italian Meatball Soup

Serves 6   *399 calories, 9 fat grams*

1 (40 ounce) can Swanson beef broth, low sodium
2 cups vegetables, diced (carrots, celery, zucchini, peas, corn, potato)
1 pound ground turkey
2 eggs
3 tablespoons Romano or Parmesan cheese, grated
1 cup Italian bread crumbs
1 tablespoon parsley, snipped

1 tablespoon onion, chopped
1 - 2 cloves garlic, minced
salt and pepper, to taste

Skim fat from canned broth and place in large saucepan. Add the chopped vegetables and heat to boiling; lower heat to simmer. Combine turkey, eggs, cheese, bread crumbs, parsley, onion, garlic and seasoning. Form into 1" meatballs. Add raw meatballs to hot soup. Cover and cook about 20 minutes, or until vegetables and meatballs are done.

"Meatballs stay round using this method, and it is quick. Serve with sourdough bread or garlic toast."
Janet Riness   **Westminster High School, Westminster, CA**

Lil's Vegetable Soup

Serves 8   *62 calories, .6 fat grams*

1/2 head cabbage, diced
1 cup French-style green beans
2 to 3 tablespoons onion flakes
2 to 3 zucchini, diced
3 to 4 stalks celery, chopped
3 to 4 bouillon cubes, vegetable, chicken or beef
1 package artificial sweetener
4 1/2 cups tomato juice
1 bell pepper, chopped
4 to 4 1/2 cups water
parsley

Combine all ingredients in large pan and simmer 4 - 5 hours. Do not boil.

"An excellent soup for those cold days or nights."
Sonja Tyree   **Ayala High School, Chino Hills, CA**

Low Calorie Creamy Potato Soup

Serves 4   *95 calories, 0 fat grams*

3 medium potatoes, peeled and thinly sliced
1 1/2 cups water
1 chicken bouillon cube
1/3 cup onion, chopped
1 cup nonfat milk
salt and pepper, to taste

Combine potatoes, water, bouillon and onions in large saucepan; bring to a boil. Cover and cook until potatoes are tender, about 10 minutes. Cool slightly. Pour into blender and blend until smooth. Return to saucepan; stir in milk. Bring to a boil and stir in salt and pepper to taste. Serve hot.

"My students love this soup, especially on a rainy winter day."
Pam Cahill   **Eureka High School, Eureka, CA**

Manhattan Red Clam Chowder

Serves 12   *140 calories, 5 fat grams*

   3 tablespoons vegetable oil
   2 cups onion, chopped
   2 cups carrots, chopped
   2 cups celery, chopped
   2 tablespoons parsley flakes
   1 (28 ounce) can tomatoes, chopped or diced
   2 cups potatoes, chopped
   1 teaspoon salt
   1 teaspoon Old Bay or seasoning salt
   8 whole black peppercorns
   2 bay leaves
   1 tablespoon dried thyme
   $1/2$ teaspoon basil
   1 quart water
   4 (6 ounce) cans clams, diced, drained (reserve liquid)

In a Dutch oven or stock pot, saute onions in oil; add carrots, celery and parsley flakes. Cook about 5 minutes, stirring frequently. Add drained tomatoes, potatoes, salt, pepper and other seasonings, In a 1 quart container, combine tomato liquid and clam liquid. Add enough water to make 1 quart. Pour liquid over vegetables. Bring to a boil. Cover, reduce heat and simmer, 45 minutes. Add drained clams. Simmer another 15 minutes. Remove bay leaf before serving.

"Wonderful wintertime soup. My family likes more potatoes, so if you increase potatoes, be sure to add more salt to your family's taste. Serve with hot French bread. Easy recipe to cut in half."
Linda Paskins   **Cordova High School, Rancho Cordova, CA**

Murphy's Tortilla Soup

Serves 12   *93 calories, 3 fat grams*

   1 bell pepper, diced
   1 cup celery, chopped
   1 cup yellow onion, diced
   2 tablespoons olive oil
   3 cups tomato puree
   $1/2$ cup green onion, chopped
   $3/4$ cup Ortega green chiles, chopped
   1 $1/2$ cups tomato juice
   2 quarts water
   1 tablespoon chicken base
   1 tablespoon beef base
   1 teaspoon oregano leaf
   $1/2$ teaspoon garlic salt

1/2 teaspoon black pepper
1 teaspoon coriander
2 1/2 cups tomatoes, diced (fresh is best)
1 1/2 cup whole kernel corn (fresh is best)
Garnish:
Monterey jack cheese, shredded
tortilla chips

Saute bell pepper, celery and yellow onion in olive oil until transparent. Add tomato puree and saute 5 minutes more. Add remaining ingredients and bring to a boil. Serve! **Note:** Garnish as desired (the cheese adds calories and fat - but, it's yummy!)

"This is a version of the soup served at Murphy's Bar and Grill in Prescott, Arizona. It has become a favorite at our house."
Joanne Vogel   Marina High School, Huntington Beach, CA

Oriental Soup

Serves 8   *313 calories, 2 fat grams*

10 cups water
1/4 pound shitake mushrooms
1 daikon radish, sliced
2 stalks celery, sliced
1 bunch bok choy, shredded
2 tablespoons burdock root
4 cloves garlic minced
2 slices fresh ginger roots, minced
3 tablespoons miso
1 teaspoon Chinese Five Spice Powder
1/2 package clear rice noodles, broken into pieces
8 ounces water chestnuts, sliced, drained
8 ounces bamboo shoots, drained
1 cup bean sprouts
1 cup snow peas
1 cup chopped spinach

In large pot, combine water, mushrooms, diakon radish, celery, bok choy, burdock root, garlic, ginger, miso and Five Spice powder; bring to a boil. Lower heat and simmer, semi-covered, for 30 minutes, stirring occasionally. Add remaining ingredients and continue to simmer 5 to 10 minutes longer, until noodles are tender. Optional: Boneless, skinless chicken breast may be added while soup is simmering to make this a main dish meal.
Becky Oppen   Dana Hills High School, Dana Point, CA

Polish Sausage Soup

Serves 9   *108 calories, 2 fat grams*

1 (15 ounce) can kidney beans, undrained
1 (14.5 ounce) can chicken broth
1 (14.5 ounce) tomatoes, diced, in juice
1 cup Pace picante sauce, mild or medium
$1/2$ pound kielbasa sausage, diced
3 cups purple cabbage, chopped
1 cup onion, chopped
$3/4$ teaspoon chili powder
1 small green pepper, chopped

In a large Dutch oven or saucepan, combine all ingredients except green pepper, bring to a boil. Reduce heat, cover and simmer 20 minutes. Stir in green pepper; simmer, uncovered, 10 minutes. Ladle into soup bowls.

"This delicious soup proves that low calorie foods are not just carrot and celery sticks. Jeanette Mortenson sent this recipe to Pace Foods, and it was published in its newsletter. It is so quick and easy and doesn't even need salt or pepper."
Gail Hurt   Estancia High School, Costa Mesa, CA

Quick Steak & Vegetable Soup

Serves 4   *316 calories, 9 fat grams*

1 pound boneless beef top sirloin steak, cut $3/4$" thick
1 ($13 3/4$ to $14 1/2$ ounce) can ready to serve beef broth
$1 1/2$ cups water
1 large onion, chopped
$1/2$ pound all-purpose potatoes, cut into $1/2$" pieces
$1/2$ pound baby carrots
1 cup frozen peas
$1/4$ cup assorted fresh herbs, chopped (parsley, chives, thyme, basil)
2 tablespoons balsamic vinegar
2 teaspoons vegetable oil
$1/2$ teaspoon coarse grind black pepper

Trim fat from beef steak. Cut steak lengthwise into three strips then crosswise into 1/2" thick pieces. In large saucepan, combine broth, water, onion, potatoes, carrots and peas. Bring to a boil; reduce heat to low. Simmer, uncovered, 15 minutes or until vegetables are tender. Stir in herbs and vinegar. Meanwhile in large nonstick skillet, heat oil over medium-high heat until hot. Add beef (1/2 at a time) and stir-fry 2 to 3 minutes or until outside surface is no longer pink. (Do not overcook.) Season with pepper. Place equal amount of beef into 4 individual soup bowls. To serve, ladle vegetables and broth mixture over beef. Serve immediately.
National Live Stock and Meat Board

Ruth Steel's Minestrone Soup

Serves 12   *179 calories, 7 fat grams*

2 tablespoons olive oil
1 pound ground turkey
1 medium onion, chopped
1 clove garlic, minced
1 quart chicken broth
1 medium eggplant, peeled and diced
1/2 to 1 cup carrots, diced
1 (28 ounce) can tomatoes, chopped and undrained
1 (15.5 ounce) can kidney beans, undrained
1 small can mushrooms, sliced
1/2 teaspoon nutmeg
1/2 teaspoon basil
1/2 teaspoon oregano
1/2 teaspoon sugar
1 large zucchini, diced
1/2 - 1 cup small macaroni
Parmesan cheese, grated, for topping

In olive oil, brown meat with onion and garlic; drain off excess fat. discard. Add broth and all remaining ingredients except zucchini and macaroni. Simmer for at least 1/2 hour, then bring to boil. Add macaroni and zucchini. Continue boiling until macaroni is tender, about 10 minutes. Serve topped with Parmesan cheese.

"This is a favorite at my mother's church. I often substitute chopped celery and green pepper for the eggplant."
Nancy Weaver   **Hughson High School, Hughson, CA**

Sopa de Fideo

Serves 8   *285 calories, 5 fat grams*

2 pounds ground turkey
2 cups spaghetti, broken
2 (8 ounce) cans tomato sauce
2 teaspoons chili powder
1 cup celery, sliced
1 onion, sliced
1 cup water
1 can corn, undrained
1 cup lowfat cheddar cheese, shredded

Using a large, covered frying pan or electric skillet, fry ground turkey and spaghetti together until turkey is no longer pink; place in colander and drain well; return to skillet. Add tomato sauce, chili powder, celery, onion, water and corn; cook, with cover on, until vegetables are tender crisp. Remove lid and sprinkle with cheese. Replace lid and remove from heat. Serve when cheese is melted.

Paula Schaefer   Garside Middle School, Las Vegas, NV

Vegetable Cheese Soup

Makes 4   *190 calories, 3 fat grams*

1 cup chicken broth
1 medium potato, peeled and chopped
1 carrot, peeled and sliced
2 stalks celery, chopped
1/2 green pepper, chopped
1/4 red bell pepper, chopped
4 broccoli flowerets, chopped
4 cauliflower flowerets, chopped
5 mushrooms, sliced
1 cup lowfat milk
2 tablespoons flour
1/4 cup cheddar cheese, shredded
black pepper, to taste

In a medium saucepan, combine broth, potatoes and carrots, Bring to a boil. Add other vegetables; reduce heat. Cover and simmer for 10 to 12 minutes or until fork tender. Stir flour into milk. Stir flour/milk mixture into saucepan. Cook and stir until thick and bubbly. Cook and stir one more minute. Stir in grated cheese until melted. Stir in black pepper.

"This would be tasty with some cooked chicken also."
Elizabeth DeMars   West Hills High School, Santee, CA

Vermicelli Soup

Serves 6   *150 calories, 2 fat grams*

1 tablespoon canola oil
1/4 cup onion, diced
1/2 of a small package vermicelli noodles
1 medium can Italian seasoned tomatoes
dash garlic
4 cups chicken stock
Lawry's seasoning salt

Coat pan with canola oil. Saute onion. Break up vermicelli in the package and add half the package to sauteed onion. Saute over low heat until lightly browned. Add tomatoes, garlic, chicken stock and seasoning salt to taste. Heat to a simmer and serve in soup bowls.

"Great with tacos or other Mexican dishes."
Yolanda Carlos   Victor Valley High School, Victorville, CA

Zucchini Soup

Serves 6   *188 calories, 11 fat grams*

5 medium zucchini, sliced
5 tablespoons green onion, chopped
4 tablespoons olive oil
4 cups chicken broth
1 ¹/₂ teaspoons curry powder
salt and pepper, to taste

Saute zucchini and green onion in olive oil until tender. Transfer to a food processor and puree. Add chicken broth, curry powder and salt and pepper to taste. Simmer 1/2 hour before serving.

"This recipe is contributed by my daughter, Ruth."
Joan Fabregue   **North High School, Torrance, CA**

Salads

Apple Cranberry Salad

Serves 10   *186 calories, 4 fat grams*

1 tablespoon cornstarch
1/2 cup sugar
1 cup water
1 teaspoon vinegar
1/4 teaspoon salt
1/4 cup nonfat evaporated milk
1 teaspoon vanilla
8 sweet apples, unpeeled, diced
1/2 cup celery, chopped
1/2 cup dried cranberries
1/2 cup pecans or walnuts, chopped
1 cup miniature marshmallows

In saucepan, mix cornstarch with sugar; stir in water. Over low heat, blend in vinegar, salt, evaporated milk and vanilla, stirring until all ingredients are dissolved. Bring to a boil. Remove from heat; cool. In large bowl, combine apples, celery, cranberries, nuts and marshmallows. Pour dressing over mixture and stir until all ingredients are coated. Chill before serving.

"This salad is a delicious variation on a Waldorf salad without the mayo!"
Sharon Turner   El Dorado High School, Placentia, CA

Black Bean Salad

Serves 10   *70 calories, .5 fat grams*

1 (15 ounce) can whole kernel corn
1 (15 ounce) can black beans
1 (12 ounce) jar thick and chunky salsa

Drain liquid from corn and beans; combine with salsa. Stir to blend flavors.

"Serve as a side dish for a Mexican meal or as a topper for baked potato. Also great as a green salad topper. The beans and corn make a complete protein, so meat isn't needed to make a meal with a potato or salad!"
Donna Love   **Quail Valley Middle School, Phelan, CA**

Chinese Cucumber Salad

Serves 6   *84 calories, 1 fat gram*

3 cucumbers
1 teaspoon salt
3 tablespoons soy sauce
2 quarts rice wine vinegar
1 tablespoon sugar
1 teaspoon sesame oil
2 tablespoons scallions, finely chopped
1 tablespoon fresh ginger root, finely chopped

Peel cucumbers; thinly slice. Mix remaining ingredients and pour over cucumbers. Stir carefully. Chill.
Carole Call   **Costa Mesa High School, Costa Mesa, CA**

Chinese Mandarin Salad

Serves 4   *273 calories, 8 fat grams*

wonton skins, cut into 1/2" strips
2 tablespoons peanut oil
Salad:
1/2 head iceberg lettuce, torn into bite-sized pieces
1/4 cup water chestnuts, sliced
1 can mandarin oranges, drained, reserving syrup
4 mushrooms, sliced
1 green onion, chopped
2 boneless, skinless chicken breast halves, grilled and cut into strips
Dressing:
1/4 cup reserved mandarin orange juice
2 tablespoons rice vinegar
2 tablespoons sugar
1/4 teaspoon garlic salt
1/4 teaspoon seasoned pepper
2 tablespoons canola oil

Heat peanut oil and fry wonton skins until crisp; drain and set aside. Combine salad ingredients in medium sized salad bowl. Garnish with crisp wonton skins. In a jar with tight fitting lid, combine dressing ingredients and shake well. Pour dressing over salad and toss lightly.

Anne Silveira   Shasta High School, Redding, CA

Crab Salad with Spinach and Feta

Serves 4   *92 calories, 4 fat grams*

- 1 1/2 ounces feta cheese
- 1 teaspoon celery seeds
- 1/8 teaspoon black pepper, freshly ground
- 1/8 teaspoon crushed red pepper flakes
- 2 cups spinach, coarsely chopped
- 8 ounces imitation crab meat
- 1 cup celery, thinly sliced
- 1 cup scallions, chopped

In a large bowl, crumble feta cheese. Sprinkle with celery seeds, black pepper and red pepper flakes. Add spinach, crab meat, celery and scallions; toss to mix well. To serve: toss with salad dressing of your choice (I like wine vinegar and olive oil).

"My favorite summer dinner - great for unexpected company."
Theresa Campbell   J. F. Kennedy High School, La Palma, CA

Crunchy Chicken Salad

Serves 3   *223 calories, 9 fat grams*

Salad:
- 1/2 head lettuce, shredded
- 1/4 cup alfalfa or bean sprouts
- 1 cup cantaloupe, musk or honeydew melon, cut into chunks
- 1/2 red bell pepper, julienne sliced
- 1 stalk celery, diagonally sliced
- 2 green onions, diagonally sliced
- 1 (5 ounce) can chicken meat
- 1 (1 ounce) package peanuts, coarsely chopped (optional)

Dressing:
- 2 tablespoons dry sherry (optional)
- 2 tablespoons seasoned rice vinegar
- 1 tablespoon teriyaki sauce

Place lettuce on serving platter. Decoratively arrange sprouts, melon, bell pepper, celery and green onions on top of lettuce. Arrange chicken over salad. Sprinkle with peanuts. Combine dressing ingredients and drizzle over salad. Garnish with additional peppers and sprouts.

Barbara Hansen   Montclair High School, Montclair, CA

Berry-Banana Breakfast Shake
1 fat gram, see page 11

Black-Bean Tortilla Pinwheels
6 fat grams, see page 11

Hearty Chicken & Rice Soup
4 fat grams, see page 22

Cucumber & Cottage Cheese Salad

Serves 4　　　　　　　　　　*63 calories, 1 fat gram*

1 medium cucumber
1 cup fat-free cottage cheese
1 tablespoon lowfat mayonnaise
1 tablespoon chives, snipped
1 teaspoon lemon juice
1/4 teaspoon salt
1/8 teaspoon pepper

Peel and dice cucumbers. Mix all ingredients together in medium bowl. Refrigerate.

Sally Engel　　　　　　　**Elsinore Middle School, Lake Elsinore, CA**

Curry Chicken Salad

Serves 10　　　　　　　　*179 calories, 1 fat gram*

1 pound skinless chicken breast halves, cooked
16 ounces bow tie pasta
8 ounces plain nonfat yogurt
3/4 cup nonfat mayonnaise
1 1/2 teaspoons curry powder
1 tablespoon lemon juice
1/2 teaspoon salt
1 cup celery, chopped
2 cups red grapes, halved

Cook pasta according to package directions; drain and rinse with cold water; set aside. In a separate bowl, mix yogurt, mayonnaise, curry, lemon juice and salt. Add chicken, celery and grapes to pasta and toss with dressing. Cover and chill.

"An easy do ahead salad."
Trena Becker　　　　　　**Ball Junior High School, Anaheim, CA**

Fat Free Vegetable & Wild Rice Salad

Serves 8　　　　　　　　*157 calories, .8 fat grams*

2 cups brown rice, cooked
2 cups wild rice, cooked
1 cup carrots, shredded
1 1/2 cups zucchini shredded
1 1/2 cups red onion, diced
1 1/2 cups water chestnuts, sliced
1 cup red pepper, chopped
1 cup green pepper, chopped
1/2 cup green onion, chopped
1 cup vinegar (balsamic, white champagne, raspberry or red wine variety)
4 tablespoons dill weed or seed

In large salad bowl, combine rice and vegetables. Pour vinegar over and sprinkle with dill weed or seed. Toss to coat and marinate for several hours before serving.

"This recipe comes from Anna Rae Conan, the computer teacher. It is so healthy, but also tastes very good."
Susan Brown   **Sowers Middle School, Huntington Beach, CA**

Fresh Summer Cucumber Salad

Serves 8   *27 calories, 0 fat grams*

    4 medium cucumbers, peeled and sliced
    3/4 cup white wine vinegar
    1/4 cup water
    1 to 2 teaspoons sugar, to taste

Place cucumbers in large jar with tight fitting lid or large bowl with lid. In a small bowl, combine vinegar, water and sugar, stirring to dissolve sugar. Pour over cucumbers and toss. Refrigerate at least 2 hours, even better, overnight.

"Yummy, crisp and refreshing."
Marilyn Tam   **Orange Glen High School, Escondido, CA**

Fresh Tomato Salad

Serves 9   *29 calories, .3 fat grams*

    4 large ripe tomatoes, cut in wedges
    1 medium sweet onion, cut in thin wedges
    1 medium green bell pepper, cut into thin strips
    3 tablespoons red wine or seasoned rice vinegar
    1 tablespoon sugar
    1 tablespoon fresh basil, finely chopped

Place vegetables in shallow dish. Combine the remaining ingredients and pour over vegetables; toss to mix well. Cover salad and chill for several hours, stirring occasionally, before serving.

"To keep the tomatoes bright and firm, make this salad nor more than 2 to 4 hours before serving."
Clyle Alt   **Bell Gardens High School, Bell Gardens, CA**

Fruit Fiesta

Serves 6   *105 calories, 1 fat gram*

    1 cantaloupe melon, halved and seeded
    1/2 honeydew melon, seeded
    1/4 cup granulated or superfine sugar
    1/4 cup fresh lime juice
    2 tablespoons fresh lemon juice

1 tablespoon orange flavored liqueur (optional)
1 ¹/₂ teaspoons grated lime peel
1 cup fresh strawberries
1 cup black or red seedless grapes

Using a melon baller, scoop flesh from melons into balls; set aside. In a large glass or ceramic bowl, combine sugar, juices, liqueur and lime peel; stir well to dissolve sugar. Add the melon balls, strawberries and grapes. Toss gently to combine. Cover with plastic wrap and refrigerate for at least 1 hour to blend flavors, stirring once or twice. Spoon fruit mixture into serving bowls and serve immediately.

"This is a cholesterol-free recipe. Melon, especially cantaloupe, is high in Vitamin A. Citrus juice adds a shot of Vitamin C."
Connie Sweet   Rim of the World High School, Lake Arrowhead, CA

Fruit Salad Berkeley

Serves 8   *104 calories, .5 fat grams*

3 pounds fresh fruit - choose seasonal fruits that are good and fresh
1 lime
Sauce:
2 - 3 sprigs fresh mint
1 teaspoon brown sugar
1 tablespoon honey
1 cup yogurt
dash balsamic vinegar

If necessary, peel fruit (such as melons). Cut into spoon-size pieces. Juice the lime and toss juice with fruit. Bruise mint with brown sugar by grinding them together until the mint uniformly darkens in color. If you have a mortar and pestle that's the perfect thing to use; otherwise, use the back of a spoon on a cutting board. Mix with honey and yogurt and add a few drops of balsamic vinegar to taste. The object is to deepen the flavor of the sauce, not make it taste like vinegar. Serve sauce over the fruit.

"My daughter, Katie, found this recipe and wanted me to add it to this year's recipe book - not only because it's good, but because of the name. As a freshman, she's looking at Berkeley as a possible college."
Brenda Burke   Mt. Whitney High School, Visalia, CA

Fruit Salad with Strawberries and Cream

Serves 4   *123 calories, 4 fat grams*

1 pint fresh strawberries, stemmed, halved, divided
1 teaspoon fresh mint, finely chopped, or ¹/₂ teaspoon dried mint
¹/₂ teaspoon honey
¹/₂ cup light sour cream
lettuce leaves
2 cups fresh fruit in season: blueberries, sliced peaches, oranges, kiwi, raspberries

To make strawberry dressing, in container of electric blender puree enough of the strawberries (about 1/2 cup) to make 1/4 cup puree; reserve remaining strawberries. In bowl, stir puree, mint and honey into sour cream to blend. To assemble salad, line individual salad plates with lettuce, Arrange reserved strawberries with other fruits on lettuce. Top with strawberry dressing.

California Strawberry Advisory Board

Greek Rural Salad (Salata Horiatiki)

Serves 8   *204 calories, 16 fat grams*

6 cups assorted salad greens
3 medium tomatoes, cut into wedges
1/2 cup green onion, chopped
1 medium cucumber, thinly sliced
1/3 cup oil (part olive, part corn)
2 tablespoons lemon juice
2 teaspoons sugar
1/2 teaspoon salt
few dashes pepper
6 ounces feta cheese
1 (2 ounce) can flat anchovy filets, drained (optional)
2/3 cup whole ripe olives, pitted
crumbled dry oregano

Wash greens, pat dry and refrigerate until ready to use. Prepare other vegetables. In large salad bowl, combine greens with tomatoes, onions and cucumber. In small bowl, mix oil, lemon juice, sugar and salt; add pepper to taste. Toss with greens. Crumble cheese coarsely and sprinkle over salad. Wrap each anchovy around an olive and place inside ring of cheese. Sprinkle oregano over all. Toss salad and serve.

"We made this for one of our international dinners, it is exceptionally good."
Janet Griffith   **Norco High School, Norco, CA**

Grilled Prawns and Spinach Salad

Serves 4   *233 calories, 9 fat grams*

1 to 1 1/4 pounds colossal prawns (13 to 15 per pound)
1/4 cup dry sherry
1/4 cup rice vinegar
2 tablespoons Oriental sesame oil
1 tablespoon fresh ginger, minced
2 teaspoons sugar
1 teaspoon soy sauce
1 teaspoon orange peel, finely grated
3 small oranges, peeled, membranes removed

3 ¹/₂ quarts spinach leaves, torn into bite-sized pieces
1 large red bell pepper, thinly sliced
salt and pepper, to taste

Peel and devein prawns. Butterfly prawns by cutting down back of each almost, but not completely through; rinse and pat dry. Mix sherry, vinegar, oil, ginger, sugar, soy sauce and orange peel. Combine 2 tablespoons of dressing with prawns; cover and chill at least 30 minutes or up to 1 hour. Reserve remaining dressing. Thinly slice orange sections crosswise, then cut in half, crosswise. In a large bowl, combine oranges, spinach and bell pepper. Cover and chill up to 1 hour. Spread prawns out flat on grill over solid bed of hot coals and grill, turning once, until opaque in thickest part (cut to test), about 3 minutes total, or use broiler and broil 1 to 2 minutes per side, until done (test same as grilling). Add prawns and reserved dressing to spinach mixture; mix lightly. Place equal portions on 4 dinner plates. Add salt and pepper to taste.

Janet Tingley   Atascadero High School, Atascadero, CA

Grilled Turkey and Corn Salad

Serves 8   *189 calories, 10 fat grams*

Marinade:
3 tablespoons olive oil
1 tablespoon garlic, minced
1 teaspoon dijon mustard
¹/₄ teaspoon salt
black pepper, freshly ground, to taste
4 turkey breast cutlets (about 1 pound total)
lettuce leaves
Salad:
1 pint cherry tomatoes, halved
2 cups corn, fresh, frozen or canned
¹/₄ cup scallions, thinly sliced
¹/₈ cup olive oil
juice of 1 lemon
¹/₄ cup parsley, coarsely chopped
salt and pepper, to taste

Combine marinade ingredients and whisk until blended. Brush on turkey cutlets. Grill about 4 minutes per side, until cooked through; or saute in nonstick skillet 2 to 3 minutes per side set aside. Line four plates with lettuce leaves. In a bowl, toss salad ingredients together. Spoon one fourth salad onto each plate. Top with sliced, grilled turkey cutlet.

"This recipe comes from Southern California Gas Company."
Angela Cruz-Trujillo   Valley View High School, Moreno Valley, CA

Honey Dijon Spinach Salad

Serves 2   ***215 calories, 1 fat gram***

1 pound fresh spinach leaves, rinsed and drained, about 8 cups
1 (11 ounce) can mandarin oranges, packed in water, drained
$^1/_2$ cup red or white onion, finely chopped
1 small red or yellow bell pepper, sliced
$^1/_3$ cup Healthy Sensation Honey Dijon dressing

In a large salad bowl, remove stems of spinach and tear leaves in half. Add mandarin oranges, onions and bell pepper and top with dressing. Toss gently and serve.

"Marsha Norton served this at a barbecue - delicious!!"
Marianne Traw   **Ball Junior High School, Anaheim, CA**

Japanese Cabbage Salad

Serves 4   ***368 calories, 14 fat grams***

$^1/_2$ medium head cabbage, thinly sliced
1 boneless, skinless chicken breast half, cooked and shredded
1 tablespoon sesame seeds, toasted
1 tablespoon slivered almonds, toasted
2 green onions, chopped
2 packages Nissan Ramen noodles
Dressing:
2 tablespoons sugar
3 tablespoons salad oil
1 teaspoon salt
1 teaspoon pepper
3 tablespoons red wine vinegar
dash sesame oil

In a large salad bowl, combine cabbage, chicken, sesame seeds, almonds and green onions; toss and set aside. In a smaller bowl, combine dressing ingredients and whisk together. Pour over salad and crumble noodles over top. Toss and serve.
Amy Filippini   **Tracy High School, Tracy, CA**

Low Fat Sour Cream Potato Salad

Serves 8   ***157 calories, 4 fat grams***

$^1/_3$ cups nonfat Italian dressing (Good Seasons)
7 medium red or white potatoes, cooked in their skins
$^3/_4$ cup celery, chopped
$^1/_3$ cup green onion, chopped
2 hard cooked eggs
1 cup fat free mayonnaise (Best Foods or Weight Watchers)
$^1/_2$ cup fat free sour cream (Knudsens)

1 1/2 teaspoons mustard with horseradish
salt to taste
celery seed to taste

Pour Italian dressing over warm potatoes that have been peeled and chopped. Quick chill in the freezer for 10 minutes. Add celery and onion. Chop egg whites and add to salad. Mash egg yolks with mayonnaise, sour cream and mustard. Add to cooled potatoes. Add salt and celery seed to taste.

"This is a good alternative to heavy fat laden potato salad. The Italian dressing's spicy flavor makes up for the difference of all the fat."
Pam Bonilla San Gorgonio High School, San Bernardino, CA

Mushroom Zucchini Salad

Serves 4 *95 calories, 7 fat grams*

1/2 pound mushrooms
1 zucchini, thinly sliced
2 tomatoes, peeled and diced
1/4 cup green onion, sliced
2 tablespoons olive oil
2 tablespoons white vinegar
1/2 to 1 teaspoon salt
1/2 teaspoon black pepper, coarsely ground
1/2 teaspoon marjoram, crumbled

Rinse mushrooms, pat dry and slice. Combine with zucchini, tomato and onion in a bowl. Combine oil, vinegar, salt, pepper and marjoram. Pour over salad and toss gently. Serve on lettuce lined plates.

"Delicious and different."
Marie Coots Huntington Beach High School, Huntington Beach, CA

Nonfat Ranch Style Dressing

Makes 2 cups *8 calories, 0 fat grams*

1/2 cup nonfat sour cream
1/2 cup nonfat mayonnaise
1 cup buttermilk
1 teaspoon onion, grated
2 cloves garlic, minced
1/4 teaspoon dried oregano leaves, crushed
1/4 teaspoon dried basil leaves
1/4 teaspoon dried marjoram leaves, crushed
1/2 teaspoon salt

Blend together sour cream and mayonnaise in a bowl. Stir in buttermilk until blended. Stir in remaining ingredients and blend well. Chill until ready to use.
Vicki Giannetti Foothill High School, Sacramento, CA

Paradise Rice Salad

Serves 5   ***239 calories, 4 fat grams***

- 1 cup white rice, uncooked
- 1 teaspoon salt
- 2 cups water
- 3 tablespoons nonfat Italian dressing
- $1/3$ cup orange juice
- 2 teaspoons honey
- $1/2$ teaspoon orange peel, grated
- 2 cups fresh spinach leaves
- 1 can mandarin orange sections
- $1/2$ cup celery, chopped
- $1/4$ cup slivered almonds

Mix rice and salt with water; bring to a boil. Cover, reduce heat to low and cook for 20 minutes; set aside to cool. Mix Italian dressing with orange juice and honey. Stir in cooled rice and add remaining ingredients. Chill before serving.

Judy Henry   **Newhart Middle School, Mission Viejo, CA**

Quick Creamy Fruit Salad

Serves 8   ***107 calories, 0 fat grams***

- 1 small package instant vanilla pudding
- 1 cup pineapple juice
- 1 (16 ounce) can chunk pineapple, packed in water, drained
- 1 (16 ounce) can fruit cocktail, in light syrup, drained
- 1 (16 ounce) can peaches, in light syrup, drained

Combine pudding and pineapple juice. Fold in thoroughly drained fruits and chill at least 2 hours before serving.

"This recipe is from my dear friend, Brenda Hudson."

Ruth Schletewitz   **Rafer Johnson Junior High School, Kingsburg, CA**

Safe Caesar Salad

Serves 6   ***321 calories, 16 fat grams***

- 3 large cloves garlic, crushed
- $1/4$ cup extra-virgin olive oil
- 3 thick slices whole wheat bread
- 2 medium-size heads romaine lettuce
- salt, to taste
- pepper, freshly ground, to taste
- 1 teaspoon worcestershire sauce
- $1/3$ cup fresh lemon juice
- 2 tablespoons mayonnaise OR liquid egg substitute
- 6 flat anchovies, drained and cut in small pieces (optional)
- $1/2$ cup Parmesan cheese, freshly grated

40

Early in the day, mix garlic and oil together; cover and set aside at room temperature. Garlic and oil should be allowed to marinate at least 8 hours and can be left to marinate up to 4 days. Preheat oven or toaster oven to 225 degrees. Remove crusts from bread and cut into 3/4" cubes. Remove garlic from oil. Toss bread cubes with 2 tablespoon oil. Spread them on a baking sheet and allow them to toast about 20 to 30 minutes, until they are golden brown, turning so they toast evenly. Remove from oven and allow to cool briefly. Remove heavy outer leaves from lettuce. Tear remaining leaves in 2" pieces. Place them in a salad bowl and season to taste with salt and pepper. Toss with remaining garlic-flavored oil. Mix worcestershire sauce with lemon juice and mayonnaise or egg substitute. Pour over lettuce and toss. Add croutons and anchovies. Toss again. Sprinkle with grated Parmesan cheese and serve.

"Wonderful recipe from the "San Diego Union". I've lowered the calories with less oil, more pepper and oregano. Try with leftover grilled chicken."
Jeri Lundy   Grossmont High School, San Diego, CA

Simple Coleslaw

Serves 6   *162 calories, 9 fat grams*

1 small head cabbage, shredded
1 teaspoon seasoned salt
1 teaspoon pepper
1 teaspoon celery seed
1/4 cup sugar
2/3 cup lowfat mayonnaise
1 teaspoon mustard
2 tablespoons wine vinegar

Wash and shred cabbage. Put in large bowl. Add remaining ingredients and stir well. Chill before serving.

"Substitute plain yogurt for the mayo. A nice alternative to a green salad."
Maria Montemagni   Strathmore High School, Strathmore, CA

Tabouli Salad

Serves 1   *257 calories, 7 fat grams*

1/4 cup dry tabouli mix
1/2 cup hot water
1 tomato, chopped
1/2 cucumber, peeled and chopped
1/4 to 1/2 cup fresh parsley, chopped
1 green onion, thinly sliced
salt and pepper, to taste

Mix tabouli and water in small bowl; let stand until all water is absorbed. Stir in chopped vegetables and season with salt and pepper, to taste.

"You can add 1 teaspoon to 1 tablespoon of oil to the tabouli mixture."
Nancy Tollefson   Poston Junior High School, Mesa, AZ

Tangy Orange Gelatin Salad

Serves 8   *127 calories, 0 fat grams*

1 (6 ounce) package orange gelatin, sugar free
2 cups applesauce
2 tablespoons orange juice or juice from 1 orange
3 tablespoons orange rind, grated
1 can mandarin orange
12 ounces diet lemon-lime soda

In a medium microwave safe bowl, mix gelatin and applesauce. Microwave on high for 5 minutes, until gelatin is dissolved. Add juice, rind, mandarin oranges, including juice, and lemon-lime soda. Blend and chill until firm.

Peg Della Zoppa   Yucca Valley High School, Yucca Valley, CA

Tortellini Salad

Serves 6   *115 calories, 3 fat grams*

1 (7 ounce) package cheese tortellini
1/2 cup parsley, chopped
1/2 teaspoon dried basil
1/2 teaspoon garlic powder
1 cup nonfat Italian dressing
1 tablespoon pimento
1 cup broccoli, chopped
1 (6 ounce) jar marinated artichoke hearts
cherry tomatoes, for garnish

Cook tortellini according to package directions; drain. Combine all ingredients and refrigerate for 24 hours. Garnish with cherry tomatoes and serve.

"It's always a hit at a picnic. Add cooked chicken for a hearty salad."
Linda Brayton   Grace Davis High School, Modesto, CA

Tropical Fruit Salad

Serves 4   *320 calories, .7 fat grams*

4 ounces Cool Whip, light
4 ounces nonfat raspberry yogurt
2 bananas, sliced
1 (14.5 ounce) can fruit cocktail, in water, well drained
4 ounces chunk pineapple, packed in water, well drained
1/2 Granny Smith apple, diced
4 mandarin oranges, peeled, diced
1 kiwi fruit, peeled, sliced
1/4 cup cherries, pitted, sliced

In small bowl, mix half the Cool Whip with yogurt; set aside. In a medium size bowl, combine half the fresh fruit with drained fruit cocktail and pineapple. Fold in remaining half of whipped topping to fruit. Pour fruit mixture into salad bowl. Frost with Cool Whip/yogurt mixture and garnish with remaining fresh fruits.

"This is a wonderful salad that could also be served as a dessert. Even young children love this dish."
Alice Claiborne   **Fairfield High School, Fairfield, CA**

Tuna Pasta Salad

Serves 6   *234 calories, 1 fat gram*

   2 cups pasta (small shells or elbow macaroni)
   1 can peas, drained
   3 to 4 stalks celery, chopped
   2 (6 ounce) cans tuna, packed in water
   1/2 cup lowfat or nonfat mayonnaise
   salt and pepper, to taste

Cook pasta in salted water until tender; rinse in cool water and drain. In a large mixing bowl, combine pasta, peas and celery, In a small bowl, blend tuna with mayonnaise. Add to pasta and stir well. Season with salt and pepper to taste.
NOTE: You can serve this on a bed of lettuce with tomato wedges and/or sliced egg. Add bread sticks for a complete "light" meal.

"I love to take this to the beach in the summer. The sea air makes the flavors come alive."
Barbara Allen   **Ayala High School, Chino Hills, CA**

Turkey Fruit Salad

Serves 4   *255 calories, 8 fat grams*

   1/3 cup plain lowfat yogurt
   1 tablespoon mayonnaise
   1 tablespoon honey
   1/2 teaspoon orange peel, finely shredded
   1/8 teaspoon salt
   2 cups cooked turkey or chicken, cubed
   1 cup chunk pineapple
   1 cup strawberries, halved
   1 small banana, sliced
   1/2 cup celery, sliced
   green leaf lettuce leaves
   2 medium oranges, peeled and sectioned
   mint leaves

In a bowl, stir together yogurt, mayonnaise, honey, orange peel and salt; cover and chill. Combine turkey, pineapple, strawberries, banana and celery. Fold in the chilled yogurt mixture, mixing lightly to coat. Cover; chill up to 2 hours. Arrange lettuce on individual serving plates. Arrange orange sections on each plate and mound turkey-fruit mixture into center. Garnish with mint leaves.

"This is a dish everyone will like - even if you're not counting calories!"
Betty Byrne   **Vaca Pena Middle School, Vacaville, CA**

Waimea Salad

Serves 8   *190 calories, 6 fat grams*

2 (20 ounce) cans pineapple chunks
2 (11 ounce) cans oranges, drained
4 cups strawberries, halved
3 tablespoons fresh lime juice
3 tablespoons vegetable oil
1 teaspoon mint
1/2 teaspoon curry powder
1/4 teaspoon salt
crisp salad greens
4 bananas, sliced

Drain pineapple, reserving 3/4 cup juice. Chill pineapple, oranges and strawberries. Blend reserved pineapple juice, lime juice, oil, mint, curry powder and salt in small bowl and refrigerate, covered. When ready to serve salad, arrange crisp greens on large serving platter. Add bananas to other chilled fruits. Attractively arrange fruits on greens. Serve with dressing.
Julie Gibbons   **Chemawa Middle School, Riverside, CA**

Winter Salad

Serves 4   *233 calories, 10 fat grams*

2 firm D'Anjou pears, peeled and sliced
2 red apples, cored, peeled and sliced
1/4 cup dried cranberries
1/2 cup pecans or walnuts, coarsely chopped
1 tablespoon lemon juice

Combine all ingredients and toss gently.

"My niece, Liz Matheny, brought this to a family dinner. It was an instant hit!"
Maridel Anagnos   **Tokay High School, Lodi, CA**

Baked Goods

Almost Fat-Free Banana Muffins

Serves 6   *130 calories, 1 fat gram*

$1/2$ cup all purpose flour
$1/4$ cup whole wheat flour
2 tablespoons brown sugar
1 teaspoon baking powder
$1/4$ teaspoon baking soda
$1/4$ teaspoon salt
$1/4$ teaspoon cinnamon
1 egg
1 ripe banana, well mashed
$1/3$ cup nonfat milk
3 tablespoons light or dark corn syrup

In a medium bowl, combine all dry ingredients. Mix dry ingredients together thoroughly. In another bowl, beat egg slightly; stir in banana, milk and corn syrup. Add liquid ingredients to dry ingredients. Mix just until flour is moistened. Spoon mixture into lightly greased muffin cups, filling each cup about 2/3 full. Bake at 400 degrees for 20 to 25 minutes. Remove from pan and eat while still warm.

"To eliminate all fat, use 2 egg whites instead of 1 whole egg. To make muffins taste really good, serve warm with LOTS of butter!"
Jan Neufeld   Fullerton High School, Fullerton, CA

Apple Dutch Baby

Serves 6   *196 calories, 8 fat grams*

2 tablespoons butter or margarine
2 teaspoons cinnamon
3 tablespoons granulated sugar
2 medium size tart apples, such as Gravenstein or Granny Smith, peeled and cored
nonstick cooking spray
3 eggs
3/4 cup nonfat milk
3/4 cup flour
powdered sugar

In a shallow 2 to 3 quart baking pan (such as a round or oval au gratin pan or a frying pan with an ovenproof handle) , melt butter over medium heat, stir in cinnamon and granulated sugar. Thinly slice apples into pan. Cook, stirring until apples begin to soften, about 5 minutes. Spray inside edge of pan with cooking spray. Place pan, uncovered, in a 425 degree oven for 5 minutes. Meanwhile, break eggs into a blender or food processor and whirl at high speed for 1 minute. With motor running, gradually pour in milk, then slowly add flour; continue whirling for 30 seconds. Remove pan from oven and pour in batter. Return to oven and bake until pancake is puffy and well browned, 15 to 20 minutes. Dust with powdered sugar, cut into wedges and serve immediately.

"A family favorite on the weekends. A giant pancake baked in the oven."
Ramona Anderson   **Mira Mesa High School, San Diego, CA**

Applesauce Pecan Bread

Serves 12   *242 calories, 11 fat grams*

1 cup flour
1/2 cup whole wheat flour
1 tablespoon baking powder
1/4 teaspoon salt
2 teaspoons cinnamon
1 cup oats
1/2 cup brown sugar
2 eggs
1/3 cup vegetable oil
1 cup applesauce
1/2 cup pecans, chopped

Stir together flour, baking powder, salt, cinnamon and oats. Beat eggs, add oil, applesauce, brown sugar and beat well. Stir in dry ingredients and nuts. Stir only until well blended, then pour into greased 9" x 5" x 3" loaf pan. Bake at 350 degrees for 1 hour.

"It could serve 18 - which would cut down the calories even more!"
Rosemary A. Ross   **North High School, Bakersfield,**

Apricot Carrot Bread

Serves 12   *166 calories, 3 fat grams*

1 ³/₄ cups flour
1 teaspoon baking powder
¹/₄ teaspoon baking soda
¹/₄ teaspoon salt
1 egg, beaten
¹/₂ cup sugar
¹/₂ cup applesauce
¹/₂ cup carrots, finely shredded
2 tablespoons vegetable oil
¹/₃ cup dried apricots, minced
¹/₂ cup powdered sugar, sifted
2 teaspoons apple juice

Preheat oven to 350 degrees. In a large mixing bowl, combine flour, baking powder, soda and salt. In a medium bowl, combine beaten egg, sugar, applesauce, carrots and oil. All at once, add dry ingredients to wet ingredients; stir just until moistened (batter will be thick). Fold in apricots. Pour batter into a greased loaf pan and bake 45 to 50 minutes or until toothpick inserted into center comes out clean. Let cool 5 minutes; remove from pan and let cool completely. Wrap loaf and store overnight before slicing. In a small bowl, combine sifted powdered sugar and apple juice; stir until drizzling consistency. Before serving, drizzle loaf with icing.

"This recipe was put out by the Mott's Applesauce people. It is not an overly sweet quick bread but has a pleasant taste due to the applesauce and apricots. My students made it for a faculty meeting and received many compliments."
Maggy Flath   Nevada Union High School, Grass Valley, CA

Banana Bran Muffins

Makes 12   *145 calories, 3 fat grams*

1 large egg, beaten
1 cup 100% bran cereal (not flakes)
1 cup ripe banana, mashed
³/₄ cup raisins
¹/₂ cup nonfat milk
2 tablespoons vegetable oil
1 cup all-purpose flour
¹/₄ cup sugar
1 tablespoon baking powder
¹/₂ teaspoon cinnamon
¹/₄ teaspoon salt

Preheat oven to 400 degrees. Lightly coat 12 muffin pan cups with nonstick cooking spray. In bowl, combine egg, cereal, bananas, raisins, milk and oil.

Let stand 10 minutes. In a medium bowl, combine flour, sugar, baking powder, cinnamon and salt. Stir into banana mixture just until combined. Spoon into prepared muffin pan cups. Bake 20 minutes, or until toothpick inserted in center of muffin comes out clean.

"I found this recipe in a magazine several years ago and have been enjoying these delicious muffins ever since. They are quick to make, very moist and keep well in the refrigerator or freezer."
Judy Banks — Temecula Valley High School, Temecula, CA

Blueberry Muffins

Makes 12 — *123 calories, 1 fat gram*

- 1 1/4 cups quick cooking oats
- 3/4 cup plain nonfat yogurt
- 1/2 cup orange juice
- 1 1/4 cups whole wheat flour
- 1/3 cup sugar
- 1 tablespoon baking powder
- 1/4 teaspoon baking soda
- 1 teaspoon dried orange rind, grated (or 1 tablespoon fresh)
- 2 egg whites, lightly beaten
- 1 cup fresh or frozen blueberries
- nonstick cooking spray
- 1 tablespoon sugar, for topping

Preheat oven to 350 degrees. Combine oats, yogurt and orange juice in a medium-sized bowl. Stir to mix well and set aside for 5 minutes. Combine flour, sugar, baking powder, baking soda and orange rind in a large bowl; stir to mix well. Add the oat mixture and egg whites, and stir just until dry ingredients are moistened. Fold in blueberries. Coat muffin cups with nonstick cooking spray and fill 3/4 full with batter. Sprinkle 1/4 teaspoon sugar on top of each muffin, and bake for 16 minutes, or until wooden toothpick inserted in center of muffin comes out clean. Remove from oven and allow to sit for 5 minutes, then remove from pan. Serve warm or at room temperature.
Gale Hooper — Casa Roble , Orangevale, CA

Chocolate Chip Orange Muffins

Serves 6 — *331 calories, 6 fat grams*

- nonstick cooking spray
- 1 cup all-purpose flour
- 3/4 cup whole wheat pastry flour
- 3/4 cup sugar
- 1 tablespoon baking powder
- 2 teaspoons orange peel, finely shredded
- 2 egg whites
- 2/3 cup buttermilk

Light & ***Delicious***

¹/₃ cup applesauce, unsweetened
¹/₂ cup chocolate chips

Preheat oven to 400 degrees. Spray six large 3" muffin cups with nonstick cooking spray and set aside. In a large bowl, stir together flours, sugar, baking powder and orange peel. Make a well in center of mixture. In a small bowl, beat egg whites until foamy. Stir in buttermilk and applesauce. Add buttermilk mixture to well in flour mixture and stir just until moistened. Fold in chocolate chips. Spoon batter into prepared muffin cups, filling each 3/4 full. Bake for 20 to 22 minutes, or until a toothpick inserted in center comes out clean. Cool muffins in muffin cups for 5 minutes, then remove and cool in wire rack. **Note:** To cut calories, make standard sized muffins, using a 12 muffin cup pan. Bake 15 to 17 minutes.

Jill Burnham   Bloomington High School, Bloomington, CA

Cranberry Orange Pumpkin Muffins

Makes 12   *85 calories, 1 fat gram*

2 egg whites
1 cup canned pumpkin
1 teaspoon vanilla
¹/₂ cup sugar
¹/₂ teaspoon orange peel, grated
2 teaspoons canola oil
1 ¹/₄ cups flour
2 teaspoons pumpkin pie spice
¹/₄ teaspoon salt
1 teaspoon baking soda
¹/₂ cup dried cranberries
nonstick cooking spray

In a medium sized mixing bowl, lightly beat egg whites until foamy. Stir in pumpkin, vanilla, sugar, orange peel and oil. Combine flour, pumpkin pie spice, salt, and baking soda in a separate bowl. Add flour mixture to pumpkin mixture, stirring until blended. Stir in cranberries. In a muffin pan, sprayed lightly with nonstick cooking spray, spoon dough into 12 equal portions. Bake at 350 degrees for 20 to 25 minutes. Remove from pan and cool on racks.

"These muffins taste great right out of the oven, or they can be stored in the freezer and warmed in the microwave as desired."
Linda Falkenstien   Morro Bay High School, Morro Bay, CA

Good For You Muffins

Makes 12   *233 calories, 9 fat grams*

1 1/2 cups rolled oats
3/4 cup whole wheat flour
1/2 cup all-purpose flour
1/2 cup brown sugar, firmly packed
3 tablespoons oat bran
1 1/2 teaspoons baking powder
1 teaspoon ground cinnamon
3/4 teaspoon baking soda
1/4 teaspoon salt
1/2 cup currants or raisins
1/3 cup dried banana chips, broken
1/4 cup pitted dates, snipped
1/4 cup walnuts, chopped
1 cup nonfat milk
1/4 cup vegetable oil
2 egg whites, slightly beaten

In large bowl, combine oats, flours, brown sugar, oat bran, baking powder cinnamon, baking soda and salt. Add fruits and nuts. Stir to coat with flour mixture. In a 2 cup measure, combine milk, oil and egg whites; add to dry ingredients and stir just until moistened. Batter will be lumpy. Spoon batter into 12 greased or lined muffin cups. Bake at 400 degrees for 18 to 20 minutes.

"The dry ingredients and fruits can be mixed ahead of time. These are great at supper time!"
Judy Betz   **Greenfield Junior High School, Bakersfield, CA**

Granny's Diabetic Delight Fruitcake

Makes 1 small loaf   *371 calories, 18 fat grams*

1/4 cup shortening
2 eggs
1 teaspoon vanilla
1/2 teaspoon salt
1/4 teaspoon soda
1/2 cup flour
1 cup oats
1 teaspoon cinnamon
1/4 teaspoon nutmeg
1/4 teaspoon allspice
1 (8 ounce) jar apricot-pineapple diabetic jam
1/2 cup walnuts
1/2 cup pecans
1/4 cup dates
1/4 cup raisins

Mix together shortening, eggs and vanilla; beat well. Sift together salt, soda and flour; add to creamed mixture. Blend in oats, spices and jam, nuts, dates and raisins. Bake in 8" ring pan or small loaf pan at 325 degrees for 1 hour, 20 minutes. **Note:** A glaze may be made by heating 4 ounces diabetic jam and pouring over cake. Top with walnut and pecan halves.

"Thanks to cousin Dianna for sharing Granny's creation!"
Rhonda Nelson   Warren High School, Downey, CA

Homemade Pretzels

Makes 4   *238 calories, 1 fat gram*

 1/2 tablespoon yeast
 3/4 cup warm water
 1/2 tablespoon sugar
 1/2 teaspoon salt
 2 cups flour
 rock salt

Preheat oven to 425 degrees. Mix together yeast, water and sugar. Add salt and flour. Place onto floured board and knead a few times. Pinch off small lump of dough and roll into desired shape. Place on ungreased cookie sheet and sprinkle with rock salt. Repeat with remaining dough. Bake 12 to 15 minutes.
Barbara Gauthier   Santana High School, Santee, CA

Low Cholesterol Cheese Pancakes

Serves 4   *168 calories, 4 fat grams*

 3/4 cup liquid egg substitute
 1 cup nonfat cottage cheese
 2 tablespoons canola oil
 1/4 cup flour
 1/4 teaspoon salt

With electric beater or egg beater, mix liquid egg substitute until nice and fluffy. In blender, blend cottage cheese until smooth; add to egg substitute. Add oil, flour and salt. Beat until blended. Bake on griddle, just like pancakes. **Note:** Serve with jam or jelly and sprinkle with powdered sugar.

"These are delicious and taste like blintzes."
Anita Huckert   Greenfield Junior High School, Bakersfield, CA

Lowfat Pumpkin Bread

Serves 24   *174 calories, .2 fat grams*

3 1/3 cups flour
1 1/2 teaspoons salt
2 teaspoons baking soda
1 teaspoon cinnamon
1 teaspoon nutmeg
3 cups sugar
1 cup applesauce
2/3 cup water
4 egg whites
2 cups pumpkin

In a large bowl, sift dry ingredients together. Make a well in the center of the dry ingredients and add remaining ingredients. Stir together until well blended. Grease and flour two loaf pans. Bake at 350 degrees for 30 minutes, then lower temperature to 300 degrees and bake for 30 minutes more.

"This recipe comes from Jared Davis."
Edna O'Neal   Durango High School, Las Vegas, NV

Miniature Fruit Muffins

Makes 36 mini or 12 regular   *130 calories, 1 fat gram*

nonstick cooking spray
1 cup wheat flour
3/4 cup all-purpose flour
1/2 cup brown sugar, firmly packed
2 teaspoons baking powder
1/2 teaspoon baking soda
1 cup buttermilk, divided
3/4 cup frozen blueberries
1 small ripe banana, mashed
1/4 teaspoon vanilla
1/2 cup unsweetened applesauce
2 tablespoons raisins
1/2 teaspoon ground cinnamon

Preheat oven to 400 degrees. Spray muffin tin with nonstick cooking spray. Combine flours, brown sugar, baking powder and soda in medium bowl. Place 2/3 cup dry ingredients in each of 2 small bowls. To one portion, add 1/3 cup buttermilk and blueberries; stir just until blended. Spoon into prepared muffin cups. To second portion, add 1/3 cup buttermilk, banana and vanilla; stir just until blended. Spoon into muffin cups. To remaining flour mixture, add remaining buttermilk, applesauce, raisins and cinnamon; stir until blended. Spoon into muffin cups. Bake 18 minutes or until lightly browned. Cool & serve.

"My favorite. These are great for breakfast."
Sandra Robertson   Whittier High School, Whittier, CA

Non-Fat Heart Breakfast Muffins

Serves 24   *85 calories, 0 fat grams*

1 cup unbleached white flour
1 cup rye flour
1 teaspoon baking powder
1 teaspoon salt
1 teaspoon baking soda
2 tablespoons sugar
1 cup rolled oats
1/4 cup molasses
1 1/4 cups nonfat plain yogurt
1 cup raisins

Sift together all dry ingredients except oats; set aside. Beat yogurt and molasses until smooth. Stir in dry ingredients, oats and raisins until blended. Let stand for 20 minutes. Grease 12 muffin cups and fill with batter. Bake at 350 degrees for 45 minutes.

"This makes a great breakfast on the run. I add extra raisins to make them sweeter."
Laury White   Fallbrook High School, Fallbrook, CA

Nonfat Harvest Muffins

Makes 36   *80 calories, 0 fat grams*

2 cups flour
2 cups whole wheat flour
1 cup sugar
4 teaspoons baking soda
4 teaspoons cinnamon
1 teaspoon salt
1/2 teaspoon cloves
4 cups apple, shredded (about 5 medium)
1 cup carrots, shredded
1 cup raisins
1 1/2 cups applesauce
1/2 cup nonfat milk
4 teaspoons vanilla
3/4 cup Egg Beaters

Preheat oven to 350 degrees. Line muffin pan with paper cup liners or use nonstick spray. Combine flours, sugar, baking soda, cinnamon, salt and cloves. Add apples, carrots and raisins; mix well. Add applesauce, milk, vanilla and Egg beaters; stir just until moistened. Fill muffin cups 3/4 full. Bake for 20 to 25 minutes, or until toothpick inserted comes out clean.

"These muffins are moist, filling and delicious!"
Cheryl McDaniels   Green Valley High School, Henderson, NV

Pumpkin-Cranberry Bread

Makes 1 loaf (14 slices)   *155 calories, 3 fat grams*

nonstick cooking spray
2 cups unbleached flour
1/2 teaspoon baking powder
1 teaspoon baking soda
1/2 teaspoon salt
1/2 teaspoon cinnamon
1/2 teaspoon nutmeg
1/2 teaspoon ginger
1/4 teaspoon cloves
1 large egg
2 large egg whites
1/2 cup brown sugar
1/4 cup granulated sugar
2 tablespoons vegetable oil
1/3 cup orange juice
1 cup pumpkin puree
1 cup dried cranberries

Preheat oven to 350 degrees. Coat a 9" x 5" loaf pan with nonstick cooking spray. Combine flour with baking powder, soda, salt, cinnamon, nutmeg, ginger and cloves; set aside. Beat the egg, egg whites, sugars and oil with an electric mixer at medium speed until smooth. Add the orange juice and pumpkin puree and beat again until smooth. Gently stir in the flour mixture and cranberries by hand until just combined. Bake in prepared pan for 50 - 55 minutes. Cool on wire rack for 10 minutes then remove from pan and cool completely.

"This makes great holiday gifts. No one seems to mind that one cup of oil is missing!"
Myrna Swearingen   **Corona High School, Corona, CA**

Spiced Granola

Serves 14   *292 calories, 14 fat grams*

4 cups old-fashioned oatmeal
1 (4 ounce) can coconut, shredded
1/2 cup raw sesame seeds
1/2 cup raw sunflower seeds
1/2 cup wheat germ
1 1/2 teaspoons cinnamon
1 teaspoon nutmeg
1/4 cup salad oil
1/2 cup honey
1 cup raisins (or dried fruit of your choice)

In a large bowl, combine oatmeal, coconut, sesame seeds, sunflower seeds, wheat germ, cinnamon and nutmeg. Add oil and honey; mix well. Pour into (2) 15" x 10" x 1-1/2" jelly roll pans. Bake at 350 degrees until golden, about 18 minutes, stirring occasionally. Cool and crumble. Stir in raisins or other dried fruit. Store in tightly covered container. Keeps best if refrigerated.

"Easy to add or delete ingredients according to your likes and available ingredients."

Nicole Hansen   Reedley High School, Reedley, CA

Sunrise Scones

Makes 32   *66 calories, 2 fat grams*

- 3/4 cup evaporated skim milk
- 1/3 cup currants
- 1 large egg, beaten
- 2 1/2 cups all-purpose flour
- 3 tablespoons sugar
- 1 tablespoon baking powder
- 1/4 cup butter, cut up
- 1/4 cup applesauce

Heat oven to 375 degrees. Spray cooking sheet with nonstick cooking spray. Combine milk, currants and egg in small bowl. Stir together flour, sugar and baking powder in a large bowl. With pastry blender, cut in butter until mixture resembles fine crumbs. Using a fork, blend applesauce into flour mixture. Stir in milk mixture. Dough will be sticky. On floured surface, knead dough lightly 4 to 5 times. Pat dough to 3/4" thick. Cut with floured 1 1/2" scalloped cutter and place on prepared cookie sheet. Reroll and cut until all dough is used. Brush tops of scones with evaporated milk. Bake 18 minutes, until golden.

Marion S. Anderson   A.G.Currie Middle School, Tustin, CA

Whole Wheat Pizza Crust

Serves 4   *341 calories, 4 fat grams*

- 1 (¹/₄ ounce) package active dry yeast
- ¹/₄ cup warm water (105 - 115 degrees)
- 1 teaspoon honey
- ³/₄ cup cold water
- 1 tablespoon olive oil
- ¹/₂ teaspoon salt
- 1 cup whole wheat flour
- 1 ³/₄ to 2 cups all-purpose flour

Stir together yeast, warm water and honey in a large bowl and set aside for 10 minutes, or until foamy. In a glass measuring cup, combine the cold water, oil and salt. Add the cold water mixture to yeast mixture. Stir in whole wheat flour and 1 3/4 cups all-purpose flour. Beat the mixture, adding more all-purpose flour as needed to make a soft dough. Knead the dough on lightly floured surface 5 to 10 minutes or until smooth and elastic. Place dough in a large, lightly greased bowl. Let dough rise, covered loosely with plastic wrap in a warm place, for 45 minutes to 1 hour. Recipe makes enough dough for one 14" pizza or 4 servings.

"Teenagers love pizza and this pizza crust supplies fiber and vitamins as well as tastes great! From Reader's Digest Live Longer Cookbook."
Nancie Wilson   **Woodland High School, Woodland, CA**

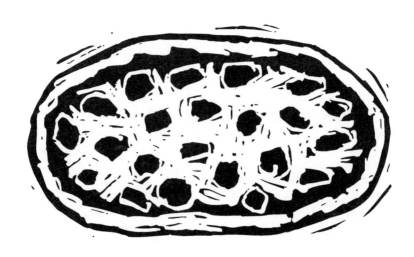

Vegetables & Side Dishes

Artichoke Squares

Serves 12   *206 calories, 5 fat grams*

2 (6 ounce) jars artichoke hearts, chopped (reserve marinade)
4 eggs, beaten
42 reduced fat Ritz crackers, crushed
5 green onions, chopped
1 pound lowfat cheddar cheese, grate

Drain artichoke hearts reserving all but 1/2 jar marinade. Chop artichoke hearts and return to marinade. Mix all ingredients together and press into 9" x 13" pan. Bake at 350 degrees for 25 minutes. Cut into squares.

"This yummy dish was brought to our house by Sue Muenster for a New Year's get together of friends."
Linda Heinbach   Yosemite High School, Oakhurst, CA

Baked Potatoes with Spiced Yogurt

Serves 8   *140 calories, 0 fat grams*

8 medium sized baking potatoes
1 cup plain nonfat yogurt
1 tablespoon fresh cilantro, minced
3 scallions, chopped, including 2" of the green tops
1/2 teaspoon powdered cumin

Scrub, prick and bake potatoes at 400 degrees for 1 hour. Meanwhile, mix yogurt, cilantro, scallions and cumin together in a small bowl. Cover with plastic wrap and refrigerate for at least one hour. When potatoes are ready, split them open and serve with a heaping dollop of spiced yogurt.

"The yogurt can also be used as a vegetable or chip dip and can be made well ahead of time. It's yummy!"
Julie Hampton   Gordon Russell Middle School, Gresham, OR

Cajun French Fries

Serves 4   *291 calories, .5 fat grams*

5 large baking potatoes, about 2-3/4 pounds
nonstick cooking spray
2 large egg whites
1 tablespoon cajun spice

Preheat oven to 400 degrees. Slice each potato lengthwise into 1/4" ovals, then slice each oval lengthwise into matchsticks. Coat a baking sheet with 3 sprays of nonstick cooking spray. Combine egg whites and cajun spice in a bowl. Add matchstick potatoes and mix to coat. Pour the coated potatoes onto prepared baking sheet and spread out into single layer, leaving a little space between. Place baking sheet on bottom shelf of oven. Bake 40 to 45 minutes, until fries are crispy, turning every 6 to 8 minutes with spatula so they brown evenly. Serve immediately.

"Great for the calorie conscious and spicy!"
Cathy Francois   Carlsbad High School, Carlsbad, CA

Chinese Broccoli

Serves 6   *125 calories, 8 fat grams*

2 pounds broccoli
1/2 cup reduced calorie margarine
1 teaspoon salt
pepper, to taste
1 (5 ounce) can water chestnuts, diced
2 tablespoon onion, minced
1/4 cup lemon juice
2 tablespoons soy sauce

58

Cut broccoli into serving pieces. Cook in small amount of water until tender; drain. In skillet or wok, melt butter; add salt, pepper, water chestnuts and onion. Cook over medium heat 2 to 3 minutes. Add soy sauce and lemon juice. Toss broccoli with sauce and heat thoroughly.

"Gives broccoli an added zest."
Janet Griffith   Norco High School, Norco, CA

Cranberry Cumberland Sauce

Makes 1 quart   *126 calories, 0 fat grams*

    2 cups whole cranberries
    3/4 cup tawny port
    1/2 cup sugar, or more to taste
    2 1/2 tablespoons orange juice
    3/4 teaspoon cornstarch
    1/2 teaspoon dry mustard
    teaspoon fresh lemon juice
    pinch ground ginger
    pinch ground cloves
    1/2 cup raisins
    1/2 teaspoon grated lemon peel
    1 tablespoon orange peel

Combine berries and port; heat over medium heat until berries pop. Add sugar and cook 1 minute. Combine orange juice, cornstarch, mustard, lemon juice and spices in large bowl; whisk until smooth. Stir in berry mixture. Add raisins and citrus peels. Return to pan, simmer until thickened. Cool, cover and chill. Serve at room temperature.

"Yummy! You may want to add a little more sugar."
Jean Hanson   Red Bluff High School, Red Bluff, CA

Cranberry Pear Relish

Serves 18   *50 calories, 1 fat gram*

    12 ounces cranberries, fresh or frozen, rinsed, drained and chopped
    1 (8.5 ounce) pear, halved and cored (leave peel on), coarsely chopped
    1 (5 ounce) orange, seeded and finely chopped
    1/4 cup walnuts, coarsely chopped
    1/2 cup sugar

Combine all ingredients together and mix well. Store covered in refrigerator. May be made 3 days ahead.

"Very easily made in a food processor. Simply chop each ingredient one at a time. Great with turkey."
Nancy Bohte   South Pasadena High School, South Pasadena, CA

Curried Rice with Raisins and Almonds

Serves 6   *230 calories, 5 fat grams*

2 cups carrots, thinly sliced
1 cup onion, chopped
1 tablespoon oil
$1/2$ cup golden raisins
4 teaspoons curry powder
$1/2$ cup stock made with vegetable flavored "Better Than Bouillon"
3 cups long grain rice, cooked
$1/4$ cup toasted almonds, chopped

Boil carrots in water until tender; set aside. In a large skillet, saute onions in oil until transparent. Add raisins, curry powder and bouillon; mix well. Stir in carrots, rice and almonds and mix, adding more stock if necessary.

"This is a great, spicy dish to compliment any meal. You can also put small pieces of chicken in this to make a main meal. My students are always surprised at the great flavors from such a weird combination of ingredients."
Lynda Waugh   San Marcos Middle School, San Marcos, CA

Grilled Vegetable Packets

Serves 4   *189 calories, 6 fat grams*

heavy duty foil
4 small baking potatoes, quartered
4 onion slices
4 green bell pepper rings
4 plum tomatoes, quartered
1 cup carrots, thinly sliced
4 tablespoons reduced calorie margarine
$1/4$ teaspoon salt
$1/4$ teaspoon pepper

Fold 4 sheets (16" x 12") of heavy-duty foil in half lengthwise. Open foil and layer 4 potatoes pieces, 1 onion slice, 1 bell pepper ring, 4 tomato pieces, 1/4 cup carrot and 1 tablespoon margarine on half of each foil sheet. Sprinkle with salt and pepper. Fold foil over vegetables; tightly seal edges. Prepare grill. Place packets on grill rack and grill 15 minutes; turn packets and cook an additional 10 minutes, or until potatoes are tender.

"An easy and unique side dish! Place carrots on top of other vegetables so they will not burn."
Debra Warren   Hueneme High School, Oxnard, CA

Lighter Green Bean Casserole

Serves 6   *131 calories, 3 fat grams*

Onion Topping:
1/2 teaspoon vegetable oil
1 large onion, thinly sliced
1/2 cup fresh bread crumbs (2 slices bread)
Casserole:
2 cups nonfat milk
6 peppercorns
1 bay leaf
pinch ground nutmeg
1/2 teaspoon vegetable oil
1 small onion, minced
1 clove garlic, minced
1/2 pound mushrooms, trimmed and sliced to make 3 cups
1/4 cup all-purpose flour
1/4 cup nonfat sour cream
1 teaspoon salt (optional)
1/2 teaspoon black pepper
1 (9 ounce) package frozen green beans

TOPPING: Heat oil. Add onions and cook for 30 minutes until golden; set aside. Toast bread crumbs in 350 degree oven on cookie sheet 5 - 10 minutes; set aside. Combine milk, peppercorns, bay leaf and nutmeg and heat on low until steaming. Let stand 5 minutes; strain into measuring cup. (Discard peppercorns and bay leaf.) In large saucepan, heat 1/2 teaspoon oil; add onion and garlic and cook 3 to 4 minutes. Add mushrooms and cook another 4 minutes. Sprinkle flour over onion/garlic mixture and stir another minute. Slowly pour in milk, stirring and bring to a boil. Reduce heat and cook, stirring constantly, about 1 minute more, until thickened. Remove from heat and add sour cream, salt and pepper. Preheat oven to 425 degrees. Assemble casserole by spreading frozen green beans into a 2 quart baking dish. Pour on sauce. In a small bowl, toss together the onions and bread crumbs and spread over the beans. Bake for 15 - 25 minutes.

"This is a very healthy alternative to the Classic Green Bean Casserole and every bit as good!"
Jan Schulenburg   Irvine High School, Irvine, CA

Non-Fat Sour Cream Topping

Makes 2 cups   *80 calories, .1 fat grams*

1 cup nonfat cottage cheese
1 cup nonfat yogurt
6 cloves garlic, minced
3 tablespoons green onion
1 to 2 tablespoons fresh herb, any desired

Place cottage cheese and yogurt in blender and blend until smooth. Stir in garlic, green onion and herbs.

"A great, flavorful nonfat topping for baked potatoes or use as a salad dressing."
Lynn Alley   **Diegueno Junior High School, Encinitas, CA**

Orange Spiced Carrots

Serves 4   ***70 calories, 0 fat grams***

1/2 cup orange juice
1 tablespoon brown sugar
1 1/2 teaspoons cornstarch
1/8 teaspoon ginger
1/8 teaspoon nutmeg
2 1/2 cups carrots, sliced
fresh parsley, chopped, if desired

In medium saucepan, combine orange juice, brown sugar, cornstarch, ginger and nutmeg; blend well. Stir in carrots. Cook over medium heat until thickened, stirring constantly. Sprinkle with chopped parsley.

"My daughter, Summer, loves these cooked carrots!"
Jeri Drake Lane   **Canyon Springs High School, Moreno Valley, CA**

Oven "French Fries" Au Natural

Serves 4   ***89 calories, 3.5 fat grams***

2 large baking potatoes
1 tablespoon salad oil
nonstick cooking spray
seasoned salt
pepper
paprika

Scrub potatoes - do not peel. Cut in half lengthwise. Cut each half into 8 crescents lengthwise with peel on each piece. Place in ice water for ten minutes to crisp. Preheat oven to 475 degrees. Drain potatoes, blot dry and toss with salad oil. Spray cookie sheet with nonstick cooking spray and place potatoes in a single layer - not touching. Bake 20 to 25 minutes turning occasionally until golden, tender and crunchy. Toss lightly with spices and serve.

"I got this recipe from Donna Swennes of El Capitan High School. My students enjoy these!"
Amber Bradley   **Granite Hills High School, El Cajon, CA**

Potato Skins (a baked French Fry)

Serves 6   *79 calories, 3 fat grams*

    4 large potatoes
    1 tablespoon olive oil
    paprika, to taste

Preheat oven to 450 degrees. Scrub potatoes well. Cut lengthwise into six wedges, the size and shape of dill pickle spears. Dry on a paper towel. In a large bowl, toss potato spears with olive oil until they are well coated. Spread on a baking sheet; dust with paprika. Bake 20 to 30 minutes, until tender.

"This recipe is quick and easy, and the resulting potatoes are scrumptious! Though it should serve 6, 2 people can easily finish them off!"
Doris Oitzman   **Victor Valley High School, Victorville, CA**

Potatoes with Mixed Garden Vegetables

Serves 4   *182 calories, 7 fat grams*

    4 (8 ounce) baking potatoes
    1 small onion, thinly sliced
    1 clove garlic, minced
    2 tablespoons butter or margarine
    1 cup mushrooms, sliced
    1 cup broccoli or cauliflower flowerets
    1 cup zucchini, sliced
    1 red bell pepper, cut into thin strips
    1/2 teaspoon salt
    1/4 teaspoon pepper
    1/2 cup light sour cream
    2 tablespoons chives, minced

Microwave baking potatoes 8 to 12 minutes on high, turning once during baking. Wrap in foil and set aside. In a 1 quart casserole, combine onion, garlic and butter. Cook on high 3 minutes. Stir in mushrooms, broccoli, zucchini and bell pepper. Cover with lid and cook on high 5 to 8 minutes, until vegetables are tender. Season with salt and pepper. Cut cooked potatoes open and fluff with fork. Spoon mixed vegetables into each and garnish with sour cream and chives.

"I demonstrate this recipe to my beginning students for their vegetable lab, and they really eat it up! Then, they prepare it the following week."
Gail C. Hurt   **Estancia High School, Costa Mesa, CA**

Sausage Mushroom Stir Fry

Serves 6   *150 calories, 12 fat grams*

3 ounces regular bulk sausage
2 ounces fresh mushrooms, sliced
2 to 3 green onions with tops, chopped
2 tablespoons butter
3/4 pound fresh beans sprouts
1 tablespoon soy sauce
1/2 teaspoon seasoning salt
1/4 brown onion, thinly sliced

Brown sausage, drain excess fat and discard; add mushrooms, onion and butter, stirring to melt butter. Add bean sprouts, then stir fry. Add soy sauce and seasoning salt to taste. Garnish with green onion tops.

"A good side dish when served with teriyaki chicken or beef and steamed rice."

Linda Robinson   Royal High School, Simi Valley, CA

Spicy Rice with Feta Cheese and Black Olives

Serves 4   *268 calories, 8 fat grams*

1 tablespoon vegetable oil
2 teaspoons garlic, crushed
1/2 cup onion, chopped
1/2 cup zucchini, chopped
1/4 cup sweet red pepper, chopped
1 cup uncooked rice
1 1/2 cups chicken stock
1 teaspoon dried oregano
1 teaspoon basil
1 teaspoon dried chili powder
1/4 cup black olives, sliced, pitted
2 ounces feta cheese, crumbled

In a large nonstick saucepan, heat oil, saute garlic, onion, zucchini and red pepper until softened, approximately 5 minutes. Add rice and brown for two minutes, stirring constantly. Add chicken stock, oregano, basil, chili powder and olives. Cover and simmer approximately 20 minutes or until rice is tender. Pour into serving dish and sprinkle with cheese.

Mary Ellen Kirk   Agoura High School, Agoura, CA

**Fruit Salad with
Strawberries and Cream**
4 fat grams, see page 35

Moo Shu Beef
7 fat grams, see page 72

Sweet & Sour Beans

Serves 4 - 6   *42 calories, 2 fat grams*

2 teaspoons sugar
2 tablespoons vinegar
4 slices bacon, cooked and crumbled
2 cans green beans

Sprinkle sugar and vinegar over beans. Heat beans in saucepan or in microwave. Crumble cooked bacon on top, toss and serve.

"Leave out the bacon to further reduce fat. This is a quick vegetable to serve after a long day at work. It has a unique flavor."
Marla Hansen   Tracy High School, Tracy, CA

Taco Seasoning Mix

Makes 3/4 cup   *32 calories, 1 fat gram*

1/2 cup onion flakes
3 tablespoons ground cumin
1 1/2 teaspoons chili powder
1/2 teaspoon cayenne pepper
1/2 teaspoon garlic flakes

Place all ingredients in a 1 pint jar; cover tightly and shake well to mix. Use to season ground beef or beans, using 2 to 3 tablespoons of the mix and 1/2 cup water for each pound of meat or beans. Store the mix in a cool, dark, dry place for up to 2 months.
Diana Lee   David A. Brown Middle School, Wildomar, CA

Main Dishes
Beef, Lamb, Pork
Poultry & Seafood

Beef Barley Stew

Serves 6 - 8   *220 calories, 4 fat grams*

1 pound extra-lean ground beef
1 medium onion, chopped
6 to 8 cups beef broth
$^2/_3$ cup barley
$^1/_2$ teaspoon dried oregano
$^1/_4$ teaspoon salt
$^1/_4$ teaspoon pepper
1 (16 ounce) can whole tomatoes, undrained
1 (8 ounce) can water chestnuts, sliced, undrained
1 (10 ounce) package frozen mixed vegetables

Brown ground beef and onion over medium heat until browned; drain. Mix beef mixture and remaining ingredients except frozen mixed vegetables in large pot; break up tomatoes. Cook over medium heat 30 minutes. Stir in mixed vegetables. Lower heat, cover, and continue cooking 30 to 40 minutes longer or until barley is done.

"Add a loaf of warm French bread and you have a wonderful, warming dinner."
Renee Paulsin   **Hemet High School, Hemet, CA**

California Pizza

Serves 4   *444 calories, 16 fat grams*

- 1 Boboli or thick pizza crust
- 4 cloves garlic, diced
- 1 tablespoon olive oil
- 6 ounces turkey breast
- 1 tablespoon crushed red pepper
- 1 jar artichoke hearts, drained and rinsed
- 8 ounces mozzarella cheese, shredded

Preheat oven to 400 degrees. Saute garlic in olive oil. Spread on prepared crust. Layer turkey breast on top of garlic. Sprinkle with crushed red peppers. Chop artichoke hearts and layer on top of turkey. Sprinkle with shredded cheese. Bake for 15 minutes, or until hot and bubbly.

"Quick! Easy! Add a tossed green salad and dinner is served."
Kris Hawkins   **Clovis West High School, Fresno, CA**

Cottage Cheese Noodle Bake

Serves 4   *348 calories, 12 fat grams*

- nonstick cooking spray
- 1/2 pound extra lean ground beef
- 1 cup celery, finely diced
- 1 medium onion, chopped
- 1 clove garlic, minced or pressed
- 1/2 teaspoon dried basil, crumbled
- 1/4 teaspoon dried oregano, crumbled
- 1/4 teaspoon black pepper
- pinch crushed red pepper (optional)
- 1 (8 ounce) can tomato sauce
- salt to taste
- 4 ounces fine or medium egg noodles
- 1 1/2 cups low fat small curd cottage cheese
- 1/3 cup Monterey jack or mild cheddar cheese, shredded
- 1/4 teaspoon paprika

Preheat oven to 350 degrees. Lightly spray a 9" x 5" x 3" loaf pan with nonstick cooking spray. Crumble beef into a non-reactive medium skillet. Add celery, onion and garlic and saute 3 - 4 minutes, just until meat is cooked. Drain off any fat and discard. Stir in basil, oregano, black pepper, crushed red pepper, tomato sauce and pinch salt. Bring to a boil over moderate heat then simmer over low heat 2 to 3 minutes, until some of the tomato sauce is absorbed into meat. Meanwhile, bring a medium pot of water to a boil. Add noodles, stirring constantly until water returns to a boil; cook thin noodles 2 minutes, medium noodles 3 minutes, stirring frequently; drain. Toss noodles in a large bowl with cottage cheese and pinch of salt. Spoon half of noodle/cottage cheese mixture into prepared loaf pan and spread with half of the meat filling. Add rest of the noodles and top with remaining meat. Sprinkle with shredded cheese and paprika. Bake, uncovered, about 30 minutes, until hot and bubbly. Let stand 10 - 15 minutes before serving.

"My mom, Patricia Odens, donated this recipe. She loves it!"
Amy Bean   Cabrillo High School, Lompoc, CA

Deluxe Pork Stir-Fry

Serves 4   *297 calories, 9 fat grams*

- 1 pound boneless pork loin
- 2 1/2 tablespoons soy sauce
- 1 clove garlic, minced
- 1 tablespoon fresh ginger root, grated
- 2 teaspoons wine vinegar
- 1 teaspoon cornstarch
- 1/4 teaspoon pepper
- 2 teaspoons vegetable oil
- 2 carrots, peeled and cut diagonally into 1/2" pieces
- 1 sweet red or green pepper, cut into 1/4" strips
- 2 small yellow squash, sliced
- 2 small zucchini, cut into julienne strips
- 1/2 cup green onions, sliced
- 6 ounces Chinese pea pods, fresh or frozen, thawed
- 2 cups broccoli flowerettes
- 2/3 cup beef bouillon
- 1/3 cup dry white wine
- 1 tablespoon cornstarch
- 1/2 teaspoon sugar
- hot cooked rice (optional)

Freeze pork for 30 to 45 minutes for ease in slicing; cut across grain into 1/4" strips. Combine 2 tablespoons soy sauce, garlic, ginger root, vinegar, 1 teaspoon cornstarch and pepper; mix well and pour over pork. Cover and marinate in refrigerator 4 hours or overnight. Pour oil around top and sides of preheated wok; heat for about 2 minutes at medium-high. Add marinated pork (undrained) to wok; stir-fry for 3 to 5 minutes. Add carrots and red pepper; stir-fry for 2 minutes. Add yellow squash, zucchini and green onions; stir-fry for 3 minutes. Add Chinese pea pods and broccoli and continue stir-frying for 2 minutes. Combine beef bouillon, wine, 1 tablespoon cornstarch, remaining 1/2 tablespoon soy sauce and sugar; pour over vegetables and pork. Stir-fry over medium heat for 3 to 5 minutes until sauce is thickened and bubbly. Serve immediately over hot cooked rice, if desired.
National Pork Producers Council

Easy Taco Salad

Serves 6   *310 calories, 11 fat grams*

2/3 cup onion, chopped
1 clove garlic, minced
1 tablespoon oil
1 pound lean ground beef
1 (8 ounce) can tomato sauce
1 teaspoon chili powder
2 tablespoons water
1 teaspoon salt
4 cups lettuce, shredded
2 cups baked corn chips
2 tablespoons green onions, chopped
1 tomato, chopped
1/2 cup low fat cheese, shredded
salsa

In skillet, cook onion and garlic in oil until tender. Add ground beef; brown, then drain well. Add tomato sauce, chili powder, water and salt to beef and cook over low heat for 10 minutes; cool. Finely shred lettuce to measure 4 cups. Place into bowl. Add chili meat mixture, corn chips, green onions, tomato and cheese. Toss and serve with salsa.

"Students love this recipe!"
Reiko Ikkanda   South Pasadena Middle School, South Pasadena, CA

Grecian Lamb Kabobs

Serves 6   *290 calories, 7 fat grams*

2 pounds boneless American leg of lamb, cut into 1" cubes
1 cup dry white wine
1/4 cup olive oil
24 bay leaves
12 pieces lemon peel, approximately 3" pieces, cut in half
2 medium onions, peeled, cut into 9 wedges, cut in half
1/2 teaspoon salt
1/4 teaspoon pepper
12 cherry tomatoes
2 green peppers, cut into 12 pieces, cut in half
Minted Orzo:
1 (12 ounce) package orzo
2 tablespoons fresh mint, chopped
2 teaspoons lemon peel, grated
salt and pepper, to taste

Mix wine, olive oil, bay leaves, lemon peel, onion, salt and pepper; place lamb in marinade. Marinate overnight; turning halfway through. Alternate lamb, bay leaves and lemon peel on skewers. On separate skewers, alternate peppers and onions; brush kabobs with marinade. Broil lamb kabobs and vegetables kabobs 5 to 7 minutes on each side. Add tomato to end of each lamb kabob during last 3 minutes of cooking. Baste with marinade throughout cooking. Meanwhile, cook orzo in boiling water for about 5 minutes. Drain and toss together with fresh mint, lemon peel, salt and pepper. Serve with lamb kabobs.

"Orzo is a Greek, rice-shaped pasta found in specialty aisles of most supermarkets."
American Sheep Industry

Grilled Lime-Marinated Pork Tenderloin

Serves 4   *372 calories, 8 fat grams*

1 1/2 pounds pork tenderloin
3 tablespoons lime juice (juice of 2 limes)
4 tablespoons vegetable or olive oil
2 teaspoons ground cumin
1 teaspoon dried oregano
2 cloves garlic, crushed
fresh jalapeno chili or 1 tablespoon crushed red pepper
1/2 teaspoon salt
pepper, freshly ground

Place pork tenderloin in a shallow, non-metallic dish or heavy ziploc bag. Combine remaining ingredients and pour over roast. Turn to coat thoroughly and marinate in the refrigerator at least 6 hours or overnight. Heat grill to medium and sear meat on all sides. Cook for about 30 minutes at medium to low heat, basting with marinade, turning every 5 - 10 minutes.

"Leftovers make great sandwiches."
Jan Hirth   Saddleback High School, Santa Ana, CA

Low Fat "Chili

Serves 6   *297 calories, 13 fat grams*

1 pound extra lean ground beef
1 medium onion, chopped
1 (29 ounce) can kidney beans, low salt, drained
1 (49 ounce) can tomato juice, or more if desired
1 (29 ounce) can tomatoes, diced
1 teaspoon chili seasoning, or to taste
1 jar medium to hot salsa (or mild, if preferred)

Brown ground beef with onion; drain any excess fat, discard. Add kidney beans, tomato juice, tomatoes and chili seasoning. Cook slowly for 25 minutes, stirring frequently. Just before serving, add salsa, to taste.

"Serve with crackers, garlic bread or breadsticks and a salad."
Rosemary Garland   Ontario High School, Ontario, CA

Mandarin Lamb With Oriental Noodles

Serves 4   *324 calories, 12 fat grams*

1 pound boneless American lamb, leg or shoulder
1 tablespoon cooking oil
2 cloves garlic, minced
1 (3 ounce) package oriental noodles, with flavor packet
1 cup water
1 small zucchini or yellow squash, cut in half, sliced diagonally
1 carrot, sliced diagonally
1/2 medium red pepper, cut into 1/8" strips
2 stalks celery, thinly sliced diagonally
1/4 cup ready to use sweet and sour sauce
1/2 cup mandarin orange slices, drained
1/4 cup almonds or peanuts, coarsely chopped (optional)

Slice lamb in 1/8" strips and set aside. Heat oil and garlic to medium-high heat in large skillet or wok. Add lamb and stir fry until lamb is no longer pink. Remove from skillet and set aside. Break up dry noodles and place in skillet with water, flavor packet and vegetables. Bring to a boil; reduce heat and cover. Simmer 3 to 5 minutes until vegetables are crisp tender. Stir in lamb strips, sweet and sour sauce and oranges. Heat through. Top with nuts, if desired.

American Sheep Industry

Maple Glazed Pork & Vegetables

Serves 5   *340 calories, 9 fat grams*

2 tablespoons butter
1 teaspoon fresh garlic, finely chopped
1/2 teaspoon salt
1/4 teaspoon pepper
1 pound pork tenderloin, sliced 1/4" thick
1 medium onion, cut into eights
3 cups cooked new red potatoes, quartered
2 medium carrots, thinly sliced
3 tablespoons maple syrup
1 (10 ounce) package frozen Italian green beans

In 10" skillet, melt butter until sizzling; add garlic, salt and pepper. Stir in pork tenderloin and onion. Cook over high heat, stirring occasionally, until pork is lightly browned, 5 to 7 minutes. Remove from skillet, keep warm. In same skillet, add potatoes and carrots. Reduce heat to medium-high. Cook, stirring occasionally, until potatoes are lightly browned, 5 to 7 minutes. Stir in maple syrup. Return pork and onion to pan. Stir in beans. Cover; continue cooking, stirring occasionally until beans are heated through, 4 to- 5 minutes.
Note: If precooked potatoes are not available, quartered raw potatoes can be microwaved. Place 3 cups quartered potatoes in 9" square microwave baking

dish. Add 1 cup water. Cover with plastic food wrap. Microwave on HIGH, stirring once, until potatoes are tender, 5 to 8 minutes. Drain before using.

Dotti Jones   Etiwanda High School, Rancho Cucamonga, CA

Mini Italian Meat Loaves

Serves 6   *224 calories, 9 fat grams*

1 (14.5 ounce) Italian-style stewed tomatoes
1 pound lean ground beef or ground turkey
3/4 cup Italian seasoned dry bread crumbs
1/2 medium green pepper, finely chopped
1/2 medium onion, finely chopped
1 egg, beaten
3 tablespoons parsley, finely chopped
1/2 cup lowfat mozzarella, shredded

Drain tomatoes, reserving 1/3 cup liquid. In large bowl, combine reserved tomato liquid with remaining ingredients EXCEPT cheese. On baking sheet, shape into six 1/2" thick patties. Top with cheese and fold over to enclose cheese in middle. Bake at 325 degrees for 20 minutes or until done. Serve topped with additional mozzarella and parsley, if desired.

Lucille Bell   Quartz Hill High School, Quartz Hill, CA

Moo Shu Beef

Serves 8   *242 calories, 7 fat grams*

1 pound boneless beef top sirloin or round steak, cut 3/4" thick or flank steak
1 cup hot water
1/2 ounce dried shiitake mushrooms (optional)
3 cups packaged coleslaw mix
2/3 cup green onions, sliced
1 tablespoon cornstarch, dissolved in 1/4 cup water
8 flour tortillas (8"), warmed
1/3 cup hoisin sauce
Marinade:
2 tablespoons soy sauce
2 tablespoons water
1 tablespoon dark sesame oil
2 cloves garlic, crushed
2 teaspoons sugar

Trim fat from beef steak. Cut steak lengthwise in half and then crosswise into thin strips. Stack 3 to 4 strips; cut lengthwise in half to form thinner strips. In medium bowl, combine marinade ingredients; add beef, tossing to coat. Cover and marinate in refrigerator 20 minutes. Meanwhile in small bowl, pour hot water over mushrooms; let stand 20 minutes or until mushrooms are softened. Drain well. Remove stems; cut mushrooms into thin strips. Remove beef from marinade; discard marinade. Heat large nonstick skillet over medium-high heat until hot. Add beef (half at a time) and stir-fry 1 to 2 minutes or until outside surface is no longer pink. (Do not overcook.) Add mushrooms, coleslaw mix, green onions, and cornstarch mixture. Cook and stir until sauce is thickened and bubbly. To assemble, spread one side of each tortilla with 2 teaspoons hoisin sauce. Spoon about 1/2 cup beef mixture in center of each tortilla. Fold bottom edge up over filling. Fold right and left sides to center, overlapping edges.

National Livestock and Meat Board

Old Fashioned Beef Stew

Serves 6   *247 calories, 5 fat grams*

nonstick cooking spray
1 1/2 pounds round steak, cubed
3 tablespoons flour
1 - 2 cups water
6 beef bouillon cubes
2 medium potatoes, cubed
4 - 6 carrots, sliced
4 ribs celery, sliced
1 large onion, sliced
2 cups peas, frozen
1/2 cup sherry or dry red wine
1 - 2 tablespoons cornstarch
2 tablespoons water

Coat a large pot with nonstick cooking spray. Coat beef with flour. Over medium-high heat, saute beef until browned. Cover with water. Add bouillon cubes. Add vegetables and sherry or wine and cook for 1 - 1 1/2 hours, until meat is tender. In a small bowl, mix cornstarch and cold water. Stir slowly into stew. Increase heat and boil, uncovered, stirring constantly for about 3 minutes. Salt and pepper to taste.

"I got this recipe from a teacher friend, Lisa Alexander. It tastes better the next day and freezes well too. Great with sour dough or corn bread."
Cari Sheridan   **Grace Yokley Middle School, Ontario, CA**

Orange Peel Beef

Serves 6   *217 calories, 9 fat grams*

1 ¹/₂ pounds lean boneless beef, top round or sirloin
2 tablespoons light soy sauce, divided
1 tablespoon + 1 teaspoon cornstarch, divided
¹/₂ teaspoon baking soda
2 teaspoon dark sesame oil, divided
2 tablespoons orange juice concentrate
1 tablespoon rice vinegar
1 tablespoon brown sugar
1 tablespoon peanut oil
3 large garlic cloves, minced
1 tablespoon fresh ginger root, minced
1 tablespoons orange peel, finely shredded (orange part only)
¹/₄ teaspoon red pepper, dried and crushed

With a sharp knife, cut beef into fine shreds (this is easier if meat is partially frozen). Combine beef shreds with 1 tablespoon soy sauce, 1 tablespoon cornstarch, baking soda and 1 teaspoon sesame oil. Mix thoroughly and let stand, refrigerated 1 to 3 hours. In a small bowl, combine orange juice concentrate, remaining tablespoon soy sauce, rice vinegar, brown sugar and remaining teaspoon cornstarch; set aside. Heat peanut oil in a wok or large nonstick skillet over high heat. Add garlic, ginger, orange peel and dried red pepper. Stir-fry for a few minutes until mixture is fragrant and starts to brown. Add beef shreds and stir-fry over high heat until thoroughly browned and just beginning to crisp. Add sauce ingredients and mix well. Cook and stir until mixture comes to a boil and thickens. Splash on remaining sesame oil, if desired and serve with rice.

"This recipe came from "Cook It Light" section of the San Diego Tribune newspaper. Tastes just like it does in restaurants!"
Adriana Molinaro   **Granite Hills High School, El Cajon, CA**

Oriental Noodles and Meatballs

Serves 6   *308 calories, 15 fat grams*

Meatballs:
12 ounces extra lean ground beef
4 ounces lean ground pork
¹/₄ cup fresh mushrooms, chopped
1 teaspoon fresh ginger root, grated
2 tablespoons green onion, minced
2 tablespoons soy sauce
1 teaspoon sesame oil
nonstick cooking spray

Noodles & Sauce:
$^1/_2$ cup condensed beef broth
$^1/_3$ cup water
1 tablespoon soy sauce
1 teaspoon cornstarch
6 ounces fresh Chinese noodles or 4 ounces dry vermicelli noodles
1 to 2 green onions

Preheat oven to 375 degrees. In medium bowl, combine all meatball ingredients. Roll heaping teaspoons into 30 meatballs, 1/2" in size. Place on cookie sheet that has been sprayed with nonstick cooking spray. Bake until lightly browned, 10 to 15 minutes. Drain off excess fat; discard. While meatballs bake, cook noodles in lightly salted boiling water until tender. Drain, rinse with hot water; set aside. In saucepan, combine broth with water, soy sauce and cornstarch. Bring to a boil, stirring constantly. Add drained noodles; stir gently until coated. Cut green onions into garnishing strips. Spoon 1/2 cup noodles onto each serving plate, top with 5 meatballs, garnish with green onion sprigs and serve.

Sheri Millhollin   Amador High School, Amador, CA

Roast Pork With Balsamic Vinegar & Sage

Serves 8   *239 calories, 11 fat grams*

3 pound pork roast, boneless, center-cut, trimmed of all but a very thin layer of
    surface fat
$^3/_4$ teaspoon salt
pepper, freshly ground
$^1/_4$ cup balsamic vinegar
2 tablespoons light brown sugar
1 tablespoon + 1 teaspoon dijon mustard
$^1/_4$ teaspoon hot sauce
$^3/_4$ teaspoon garlic, minced
$^1/_3$ cup beef broth
1 $^1/_2$ tablespoons butter
1 tablespoon sage, minced
sage sprigs

Season entire surface of pork with salt and pepper to taste. Put in shallow roasting pan lined with foil. Roast, uncovered, at 375 degrees for 30 minutes. While pork is roasting, combine vinegar, brown sugar, mustard, hot sauce and garlic in small bowl to make basting liquid. Reserve 3 tablespoons for sauce. After 30 minutes of roasting, pour off drippings so fat has time to separate out from pan juices. Baste meat with vinegar mixture. Roast until meat registers 170 degrees, about 35 minutes more, basting meat often with vinegar mixture. Transfer meat to warm platter and tent with foil until sauce is finished. Bring reserved 3 tablespoons vinegar mixture, beef broth and skimmed pan juices to boil in small nonstick skillet. Simmer, uncovered, until slightly thickened, about 5 minutes. Stir in butter until melted. Taste and

Light & ***Delicious***

adjust seasonings; lower heat to keep warm. Transfer meat to cutting board. Slice meat into thin slices. Arrange slices, overlapping on platter. Add any meat juices to sauce, then drizzle sauce over meat. Sprinkle with minced sage. Garnish with sage springs. Serve hot.

"Balsamic vinegar sauce is outstanding!"
Helen Lievre   La Cañada High School, La Cañada, CA

Sesame Pork with Curried Rice

Serves 6   ***327 calories, 4 fat grams***

2 cups water
1 cup uncooked rice
1 1/4 cups orange juice, divided
1 tablespoon + 1 teaspoon low-sodium soy sauce, divided
1 pound pork, cut in 1/2" strips
nonstick cooking spray
1/2 teaspoon curry powder
1/4 teaspoon salt
1/4 cup rice vinegar
2 tablespoons lemon juice
1 tablespoon dark sesame oil
1 teaspoon dijon mustard
1 teaspoon honey
1 clove garlic
1/2 cup celery, sliced
1/2 cup radishes, sliced
1/2 cup cilantro, chopped
1/3 cup snow peas, sliced diagonally
1/3 cup green onions, slivered
1/4 teaspoon hot chili pepper seeds
2 teaspoons ginger, grated

In 8 cup measuring cup, cook rice and water in microwave oven for 10 minutes on high. Let stand for 5 - 10 minutes. Do not drain off extra water - it will be absorbed. Meanwhile, combine 1/4 cup orange juice and 1 teaspoon soy sauce; stir well. Place pork on a broiler rack coated with cooking spray. Brush orange juice mixture over pork. Broil 3 inches from heat 5 minutes on each side or until done, basting occasionally with orange juice mixture. Combine remaining 1 cup orange juice with curry powder, salt, vinegar, lemon juice, sesame oil, 1 tablespoon soy sauce, dijon mustard, honey and garlic. Stir well. Add pork and rice; stir well. Let stand 10 minutes. Add remaining ingredients; toss well.

"This may be garnished with toasted sesame seeds, but will add fat grams!"
Tricia Montelongo   South Junior High School, Anaheim, CA

Skinny Chili

Serves 8   *256 calories, 12 fat grams*

1 pound lean ground beef
1 medium onion, diced
2 cups celery, sliced
1/2 cup green pepper, diced
1/2 teaspoon garlic salt
1 (15 ounce) can kidney beans, undrained
2 (1 pound) cans tomatoes
1 tablespoon chili powder
1 bay leaf
salt, to taste
tabasco, to taste

Brown ground beef with onion; drain off fat; discard. Add remaining ingredients. Simmer, covered, for 2 hours. Serve hot with crackers.

"Yum! Warms you up and makes you feel healthy!"
Debbie Rothe   **Alta Loma High School, Alta Loma, CA**

Slim Spaghetti and Meatballs

Serves 4   *410 calories, 11 fat grams*

Meatballs:
1/2 pound extra lean ground beef
1/8 cup fresh parsley, chopped
1 tablespoon onion, diced
1/2 teaspoon whole leaf oregano, crumbled
1/2 teaspoon salt
Sauce:
1 (15 ounce) can whole tomatoes
1 (6 ounce) can tomato paste
1 cup water
1 clove garlic, minced
1/4 cup onion, diced
1/4 teaspoon oregano
1/4 teaspoon salt
dash pepper
pinch cayenne pepper
8 ounces spaghetti, cooked

Combine beef, parsley, 1 tablespoon minced onion, oregano and 1/2 teaspoon salt; shape into meatballs about the size of a walnut. Broil 3 inches from heat about 5 minutes on each side, until browned; set aside. In large saucepan, combine remaining ingredients, except pasta, and bring to a boil. Reduce heat, add meatballs and simmer for 30 to 40 minutes. Serve over cooked spaghetti.

"We do this recipe in our low calorie unit, and the students really like it."
Joanne Montoy   **Esperanza High School, Anaheim, CA**

Taco Potatoes

Serves 1   *249 calories, 12 fat grams*

1 small russet potato
2 tablespoons light sour cream
1 teaspoon taco seasoning
2 - 3 tablespoons taco meat, cooked
1/4 cup lettuce or cabbage, shredded
2 tablespoons cheese, shredded
salsa

Bake potato conventionally or in the microwave. Slice open; lay flat. Mix sour cream and taco seasoning together. Spread over potato. Sprinkle with meat, shredded lettuce and cheese. Top with salsa. NOTE: Can also be made without meat!

"I originally made up this recipe after a leftover taco dinner. Now it is a family favorite as well as a hit in my Beginning Foods class."
Nanci Burkhart   **Hueneme High School, Oxnard, CA**

25 Garlic Clove Chicken

Serves 4   *316 calories, 9.5 fat grams*

nonstick cooking spray
2 pounds meaty chicken pieces (breasts, thighs, drumsticks), skin removed
25 cloves garlic (approx. 2-3 bulbs), unpeeled
1/4 cup dry white wine or 1/4 cup chicken bouillon
4 teaspoons lemon juice
salt and ground red pepper

Spray a large skillet with nonstick cooking spray. Preheat skillet over medium heat. Add chicken and saute for 10 minutes, turning to brown evenly. Place chicken in an 8" x 8" x 2" or 10" x 6" x 2" baking dish. Add unpeeled garlic cloves. In a small bowl, combine wine or bouillon and lemon juice; pour over chicken. Lightly sprinkle chicken with salt and ground red pepper. Bake, covered, in a 325 degree oven for 45 to 50 minutes, or until tender.

"This is from 'Better Homes & Gardens'. Don't eat all the garlic!"
Kathy Croxall   **Fontana High School, Fontana, CA**

Arroz Con Pollo

Serves 6   *330 calories, 5 fat grams*

1 (16 ounce) can tomatoes
1 1/2 cups chicken broth
1 teaspoon salad oil
3 pounds chicken, cut up
1 onion, chopped

1 green pepper, chopped
1 clove garlic, minced
1 cup long grain rice
1 teaspoon dried oregano
1/4 teaspoon ground cumin
1/4 teaspoon pepper
1 bay leaf
1 package frozen peas
salt, to taste
1/4 cup green onion, sliced

Drain liquid from tomatoes; add enough broth to liquid to make 2 cups; set aside. Heat oil in fry pan over medium-high heat. Cook chicken until browned on all sides. Add water, 1 tablespoon at a time, if pan appears dry. Discard all but 1 teaspoon of the drippings. Add onion, bell pepper and garlic to pan; cook, stirring until onion is soft. Stir in tomatoes, broth mixture, rice, oregano, cumin, pepper and bay leaf. Bring to a boil. Return chicken to pan. Reduce heat, cover and simmer until chicken is cooked, about 45 minutes. Stir in peas, season with salt. Garnish with green onion.

Brenda Umbro   Orange Glen High School, Escondido, CA

Baked Lemon-Pepper Chicken

Serves 4   *178 calories, 3 fat grams*

nonstick cooking spray
1 to 2 onions, thinly sliced
4 skinless chicken breast halves
1 teaspoon lemon pepper
1 tablespoon Parmesan cheese, grated
1 teaspoon basil

Preheat oven 400 degrees. Spray a casserole dish with nonstick cooking spray; spread onions all over bottom. Place chicken breasts on top, bone side down and sprinkle with lemon pepper, Parmesan cheese, and basil. Bake, uncovered, about 1 hour.

"So easy - put some potatoes in to bake at the same time! Freezes well."
Saralee Kroll   Alta Loma High School, Alta Loma, CA

Baked Sweet and Sour Chicken Breasts

Serves 8   *178 calories, 1 fat gram*

1/2 cup orange marmalade
1/2 envelope onion soup mix
1/2 cup green pepper, chopped
1/2 teaspoon light soy sauce
3/4 cup orange juice
1/4 cup fat free Italian dressing
8 boneless, skinless chicken breast halves

I̶n small bowl, combine marmalade, onion soup mix, green pepper, soy sauce, orange juice and Italian dressing. Spray large pan or dish with nonstick cooking spray. Place chicken breasts on pan and pour sauce over. Bake at 350 degrees for 40 to 45 minutes.

"Fast, easy to make and tasty."
Karen Frontino   **Arcadia High School, Arcadia,**

Brunswick Stew

Serves 6   ***255 calories, 5 fat grams***

- 1 tablespoon olive oil
- 1 medium onion, chopped
- 1 pound boneless, skinless chicken breast halves, cut into 1" cubes
- 1 1/2 cups tomatoes, chopped
- 1 (6 ounce) can no salt-added tomato paste
- 10 ounces baby lima beans, fresh or frozen
- 3 cups chicken stock, homemade
- 1 tablespoon worcestershire sauce
- 3 tablespoons fresh lemon juice

I̶n deep skillet or Dutch oven, heat oil over medium-high heat. Add onion and saute until soft, about 3 minutes. Add chicken pieces and remaining ingredients. Reduce heat to low and simmer 1 hour.

"The Brunswick Stew is just an old Southern favorite."
Cora Lynn Woodall   **Green Valley High School, Henderson, NV**

California Apricot Mixed Grill

Serves 4   ***303 calories, 6 fat grams***

- 4 skinless chicken breast halves
- 4 cloves garlic, peeled, roughly chopped
- 1/4 teaspoon salt
- 1/4 teaspoon black pepper
- 2 small red onions, sliced 1/3" thick
- 6 fresh California apricots, halved and pitted
- *Vinaigrette:*
- 2 tablespoons California apricot nectar
- 2 tablespoons balsamic vinegar
- 1 tablespoon olive oil
- salt and pepper, to taste
- 4 cups mixed salad greens, rinsed and dried

U̶p to 12 hours ahead, combine chicken and garlic; season with salt and pepper. Cover and refrigerate until ready to grill. In small bowl, combine nectar and vinegar; whisk in olive oil to emulsify. Season with salt and pepper; set aside. Grill chicken 4 minutes on each side or just until cooked through. While chicken is grilling, grill onion; grill about 2 minutes on each side. Brush

apricots lightly with oil; grill about 1 minute on each side. Toss greens with vinaigrette; top with mixed grill.
California Apricot Advisory Board

Chicken Breast Veronique

Serves 8   *322 calories, 11 fat grams*

8 skinless chicken breast halves
1 cup cracker crumbs (made from low or nonfat crackers)
1/2 teaspoon salt
1/4 teaspoon pepper, freshly ground
1/2 teaspoon dried tarragon
pinch nutmeg
nonstick cooking spray
2 tablespoons margarine
1/4 cup onion, chopped
1/2 cup chicken broth
1/2 cup dry white wine or vermouth
2 cups mushrooms, sliced
2 cups seedless green grapes

Combine cracker crumbs, salt, pepper, tarragon and nutmeg. Coat chicken in this mixture. Melt 1 tablespoon margarine in a skillet that has been sprayed with nonstick cooking spray. Brown chicken on both sides. Remove chicken, place in a single layer in a shallow baking pan. Preheat oven to 375 degrees. Add onions to skillet and saute until transparent. Drain off any excess oil. Pour in broth and wine; bring to boil. Pour around the chicken. Bake uncovered, for 30 minutes. While chicken is baking, melt 2 teaspoons margarine in a skillet, Saute mushrooms until tender. Arrange mushrooms and grapes around chicken. Bake 8 to 10 minutes longer or until chicken is tender.

"I often serve this dish to guests and never tell them it is a "heart healthy" recipe - until they ask for the recipe - then they are always surprised that something so good is good for them!"
Kathleen Bobczynski   Mira Mesa High School, San Diego, CA

Chicken Bundles Italian

Serves 8   *227 calories, 10 fat grams*

2 boneless, skinless chicken breasts, chopped (about 1 1/2 cups)
1 cup onion, chopped
1 tablespoon olive oil
1 (10 ounce) package frozen spinach, thawed and drained
1 cup lowfat ricotta cheese
1/3 cup Parmesan cheese
1/2 teaspoon garlic powder
1/4 teaspoon dried oregano, crushed
1/4 teaspoon ground nutmeg
1/4 teaspoon lemon juice
salt and pepper, to taste
8 (7") egg roll wrappers
2 tablespoons margarine, melted
nonstick cooking spray

In a large skillet, cook chicken and onion in hot oil over medium heat until chicken is no longer pink and onion is tender. In a large mixing bowl, combine spinach, ricotta cheese, Parmesan cheese, garlic powder, oregano, nutmeg and lemon juice. Stir in chicken and onions; season to taste with salt and pepper. Spray 8 (10 ounce) custard cups with nonstick cooking spray. Line each cup with an egg roll wrapper. Divide chicken mixture among the 8 dishes. Fold the ends of each wrapper over the top of the chicken mixture, sealing to make a bundle. Brush with melted margarine. Bake at 350 degrees for 20 to 25 minutes or until tops are golden. To serve, loosen bundles with a knife and remove from cups.

"Using a lowfat filling of ricotta cheese, spinach and chicken, cuts calories but not flavor."
Julie Shelburne   Tulare Union High School, Tulare, CA

Chicken Cacciatore

Serves 6   *209 calories, 2 fat grams*

4 boneless, skinless chicken breast halves or 1 cut up fryer, skin removed
1 large onion, chopped or sliced
1 clove garlic, minced
2 to 3 cups canned tomatoes
1 teaspoon oregano
1/2 teaspoon salt
pepper to taste
2 cups cooked brown rice, noodles or potatoes

Place chicken in a heavy pan or skillet. Combine remaining ingredients (except rice, noodles or potatoes) and pour over chicken. Cover and steam about 1 hour. If desired, uncover during last 15 minutes of cooking to thicken sauce. Serve over rice, noodles or potatoes. **Note:** Carrots and potatoes may be cooked along with chicken in sauce, if desired. **Microwave directions:** Use a 7" x 9" or 9" x 13" baking dish. Cover with waxed paper, cook at 80% power for 28-32 minutes, until meat near bone is no longer pink. Turn twice during cooking.

"Quick, easy and delicious. Great company dish. No one knows they are eating lowfat."
Susan Eckert   Basic High School, Henderson, NV

Chicken Cheese Dijon

Serves 4   *215 calories, 3 fat grams*

    4 boneless, skinless chicken breast halves
    1 tablespoon dijon mustard
    1 medium onion, finely chopped
    1 cup lowfat Swiss cheese, grated

Place chicken breasts on a cookie sheet covered with aluminum foil. Spread dijon mustard evenly on each breast and sprinkle with onion. Cover each with grated Swiss cheese. Bake at 350 degrees for 25 minutes.

"Everyone always wants this recipe because it's delicious, easy and low in calories."
Angela Croce   Mira Mesa High School, San Diego, CA

Chicken Enchiladas

Serves 8   *220 calories, 5 fat grams*

    2 boneless, skinless chicken breasts
    3 stalks celery, cut into chunks
    1 medium onion, cut into chunks
    2 cloves garlic
    1 1/2 cups chicken stock or canned broth
    Filling:
    1/2 medium green pepper, diced
    1/2 medium white onion, diced
    1 large tomato, diced
    1 (3.5 ounce) can whole green chiles, diced
    1/4 cup chicken stock or canned broth
    1/4 teaspoon salt
    1/4 teaspoon black pepper
    8 flour or corn tortillas
    2 ounces part-skim mozzarella cheese, thinly sliced
    1/2 cup enchilada sauce

In a medium stockpot, combine chicken, celery, onion chunks, garlic and chicken stock or broth and bring to a boil. Cover, reduce heat and simmer 30 minutes. Remove from heat. Let sit in stock 15 minutes. Remove celery, onion and garlic from stock and discard. Reserve remaining stock for later use. Tear chicken into strips. To prepare filling: in medium stockpot, combine green pepper, diced onion, tomato, green chiles, 1/4 cup chicken stock, salt and pepper. Cook over low heat 20 minutes or until vegetables are soft. Add chicken. To assemble: place 1/4 cup filling in each tortilla, along with a thin slice of mozzarella cheese and 1 teaspoon enchilada sauce. Roll and place seam side down in a lightly greased 9" x 13" ovenproof baking dish. Pour remaining enchilada sauce over top. Cover with foil and bake at 350 degrees for 20 to 25 minutes. Serve with tomato salsa.

"I used this recipe in a comparison taste test. Half the kitchens prepared a traditional high calorie chicken enchilada recipe with cheddar cheese, while the other half made the lower calorie enchilada recipe above. Surprisingly, the lower calorie version won!"
JoAnn Coleman   **Santa Ana High School, Santa Ana, CA**

Chicken Pot Pie

Serves 4   *468 calories, 14 fat grams*

1 cup chicken broth
3 medium carrots, cut into 1/2" chunks
2 medium potatoes, cubed
1 pound chicken breast meat, cut into 1" pieces
1/2 cup evaporated skim milk
3 tablespoons flour
1/2 teaspoon sage
1/2 teaspoon salt
1/4 teaspoon pepper
1 cup frozen pearl onions
1 cup frozen peas
2 17"x11" phyllo sheets, cut crosswise in half

Preheat oven to 375 degrees. In saucepan, combine broth, carrots, potatoes and chicken pieces; simmer until tender. In another saucepan, combine evaporated skim milk, flour, sage, salt and pepper. Boil, then reduce heat to simmer until consistency of heavy cream. Stir in chicken mixture, pearl onions and peas and cook for 1 minute longer. Spoon mixture into deep dish pie pan or 8" x 8" glass casserole dish. Layer phyllo sheets on top. Cut a 3" X on top and fold back. Bake pie for 10 to 15 minutes or until filling is heated through and phyllo dough is crisp and browned.
Myra Skidmore   **Downey High School, Downey, CA**

Chicken Soft Tacos

Serves 4   *304 calories, 13 fat grams*

1 cup chicken, cooked and shredded
1/3 cup water
1 teaspoon dried onion
1/4 teaspoon dried garlic
1 teaspoon chili powder
1/4 teaspoon salt

¹/₄ teaspoon ground cumin
4 flour tortillas
¹/₂ cup lettuce, shredded
¹/₂ cup cheddar cheese, shredded
Optional:
¹/₂ tomato, chopped
¹/₄ cup sour cream
¹/₄ cup picante sauce

Cook chicken, water, onion, garlic, chili powder, salt and cumin in saucepan over medium heat for 5 to 10 minutes. Wrap flour tortillas in damp cloth and heat in microwave 1 minute on high power. Spoon 1/4 cup chicken mixture into each tortilla. Top with lettuce and cheese and, if desired, optional items.

Patty Stroming-Jaquith   Mitchell Sr. Elementary, Atwater, CA

Chicken Spaghetti

Serves 4   *395 calories, 9 fat grams*

¹/₂ cup onion, minced
1 clove garlic, minced
2 teaspoons reduced calorie margarine
4 boneless, skinless chicken breast halves
1 (15 ounce) can tomatoes, pureed
1 (8 ounce) can tomato sauce
1 teaspoon basil
¹/₄ teaspoon thyme
¹/₄ teaspoon Italian seasoning
¹/₂ teaspoon salt
¹/₂ teaspoon pepper
4 cups spaghetti, cooked

In a 10" nonstick skillet, saute onion and garlic in margarine until lightly browned. Cut each chicken breast into 8 pieces. Brown breasts with onion and garlic. Add tomatoes and sauce; bring to a boil. Reduce heat and add seasonings, salt and pepper. Cover and simmer until chicken is tender, 20 - 30 minutes. Serve over hot cooked spaghetti.

"My family loves sliced black olives and Parmesan cheese added, but they really add a lot more calories and fat!"
DeLisa Davis   Sutter High School, Sutter, CA

Chicken Stir-Fry

Serves 4   *153 calories, 3.5 fat grams*

1 tablespoon oil
3/4 pound broccoli, chopped
5 to 6 stalks celery, chopped
1/2 onion, sliced
2 carrots, sliced
4 ounces mushrooms, sliced
1 green pepper, sliced
12 ounces chicken breast, cooked, cut into 1" pieces
2 chicken bouillon cubes
1 cup water
4 tablespoons soy sauce
2 teaspoons sugar
2 tablespoons cornstarch
2 cups rice, cooked

In large skillet or wok, stir fry vegetables in oil until tender crisp; add cooked chicken and heat through. While vegetables are cooking, in a small saucepan dissolve bouillon cubes in 1/2 cup warm water. Bring to a boil, then add soy sauce and sugar. Mix cornstarch and remaining 1/2 cup water together then add to boiling mixture; stir until thickened. Pour over stir fried vegetables and chicken, tossing to coat with sauce. Serve over cooked rice.

"One of my favorite meals, and I'm skinny!"
Sue Fullmer   Durango High School, Las Vegas, NV

Chicken Tidbits

Serves 2   *195 calories, 4 fat grams*

2 boneless, skinless chicken breast halves, cubed
1/4 cup bread crumbs
1 tablespoon Parmesan cheese, grated
1/4 teaspoon salt

Combine bread crumbs, Parmesan cheese and salt in a bowl. Roll each chicken tidbit in the bread crumb mixture, covering completely. Place 12 tidbits on a dish, in ring formation and microwave on high for 2 minutes, turning once during cooking. Repeat with remaining tidbits.

"A favorite with my kids, Andrea and Matthew!"
Gaylen Roe   Magnolia Junior High School, Chino, CA

Chicken with Salsa Stuffing

Serves 4   *340 calories, 4.5 fat grams*

3/4 cup hot water
2 cups stuffing mix
3/4 cup salsa

4 boneless, skinless chicken breast halves

Combine water with stuffing mix; add 1/4 cup salsa. Spread stuffing in 9" x 9" baking dish. Place chicken on top of stuffing and pour over remaining 1/2 cup salsa. Cover dish with foil and bake at 350 degrees for 40 minutes, or until chicken is cooked through.

"Add a green salad, and you have a quick and easy meal."
Sue Waterbury   San Luis Obispo High School, San Luis Obispo, CA

Chimichangas

Serves 12   *386 calories, 18 fat grams*

1 medium onion, chopped
1 small can diced green chiles
2 1/2 to 3 pounds chicken or turkey breast meat, shredded
1/2 can tomatoes, drained and diced
oregano, to taste
salt, to taste
pepper, to taste
1 tablespoon sugar
12 flour tortilla, medium sized
1/4 cup margarine
1-1/2 cups lowfat cheddar cheese, shredded

Saute onion and green chilies in 1 teaspoon water. Add shredded chicken or turkey and drained tomatoes; simmer 30 to 60 minutes. Add seasonings to taste and sugar. While filling is simmering, lightly butter both sides of tortillas. Fill each tortilla with about 1/4 cup filling, top with 2 tablespoons shredded cheese; roll burrito-style. Place seam side down on cookie sheet and bake at 350 degrees for 15 to 18 minutes.

"Beef from a chuck roast can be substituted for chicken. These are great ways to use up leftover turkey at Thanksgiving. Lowfat tortillas will reduce fat content further!"
Joan Goodell   Eldorado High School, Las Vegas, NV

Coach Sullivan's Chicky Stroganoff

Serves 4   *404 calories, 3 fat grams*

- 1/2 medium onion, chopped
- 2 cups mushrooms, sliced
- 2 chicken bouillon cubes
- 2 bay leaves
- 1/8 teaspoon garlic powder
- 1/8 teaspoon pepper
- 1 tablespoon dried parsley
- 1/2 teaspoon Kitchen Bouquet
- 1/3 cup water
- 1 tablespoon + 1 teaspoon cornstarch
- 4 tablespoons cold water
- 1 1/2 pounds chicken, cooked and diced
- 1/2 cup plain lowfat yogurt
- 2 cups rice or noodles, cooked

In a large fry pan, simmer onion, mushrooms, bouillon, bay leaves, garlic powder, pepper, dried parsley, Kitchen Bouquet and 1/3 cup water together until onions are transparent, about 3 to 5 minutes. In a small bowl, dissolve cornstarch in 4 tablespoons cold water; add to vegetables and stir until thickened. Add chicken; simmer 2 minutes more. Stir in yogurt and simmer 2 minutes more. Serve over hot rice or noodles.

"Enjoy the great carbos."
Debbie Sullivan   **Silverado High School, Las Vegas, NV**

Crusty Calzone

Serves 8   *230 calories, 7 fat grams*

- 1 pound frozen bread dough, thawed to room temperature
- nonstick cooking spray
- 1/4 cup pizza sauce
- 1/2 teaspoon garlic powder
- 1/4 teaspoon Italian herb seasoning
- 1/2 pound turkey smoked sausage, thinly sliced
- 1/2 onion, sliced
- 1 green pepper, sliced
- 4 ounces lowfat mozzarella or cheddar cheese, grated

Ground Beef or Turkey Variation:

- 1/2 pound extra lean ground beef or turkey, cooked and crumbled
- 1 cup vegetables, sliced
- 4 ounces lowfat cheese, grated

Turkey Ham Variation:

- 1/2 pound turkey ham, sliced
- 1/2 cup pineapple chunks, unsweetened and drained
- 4 ounces lowfat cheese, grated

Sliced Turkey Variation:
  ¹/₂ pound turkey, sliced
  ¹/₂ cup mushrooms, sliced
  4 ounces lowfat cheese, grated

Preheat oven to 425 degrees. Roll dough into 10" x 14" rectangle and place on baking sheet that has been sprayed with nonstick cooking spray. Spread pizza sauce on half of the dough and sprinkle with seasonings. Top with smoked sausage, onion, green pepper and cheese. Fold dough over and press edges together to seal filling. Bake 20 minutes. Allow to cool 5 minutes before cutting to serve.

Gerri Hickman   **Grant Sawyer Middle School, Las Vegas, NV**

Fiesta Chicken

Serves 4   *487 calories, 13 fat grams*

  2 tablespoons oil
  4 cloves garlic, minced
  1 ¹/₄ pounds boneless, skinless chicken, cut into 1 ¹/₂" pieces
  ¹/₄ teaspoon salt
  1 teaspoon chili powder
  1 (14 ¹/₂ ounce) can stewed tomatoes, with juice
  1 (10 ounce) package frozen green beans
  1 (4 ounce) can green chilies, drained
  2 (1 ounce) squares semi-sweet chocolate, coarsely chopped
  ¹/₂ teaspoon ground cinnamon
  3 tablespoons cilantro, freshly minced
  1 tablespoon lime juice

Heat oil in a Dutch oven over moderate heat for 1 minute. Add garlic and saute, stirring frequently for 2 minutes. Add chicken and salt; saute about 5 minutes. Stir in chili powder and cook for 1 minute. Add the tomatoes (breaking them up with a spoon), beans, chilies, chocolate, cinnamon and cilantro; bring to a boil. Reduce heat to low and simmer until sauce has thickened and chicken is no longer pink, 10 to 15 minutes. Stir in lime juice. Serve with tortillas.

"For parties, serve with sour cream, sliced avocado and black beans."
Ava Smalley   **La Puente High School, La Puente, CA**

Greek Chicken with Cheese

Serves 6   ***366 calories, 15 fat grams***

1 tablespoon olive oil
6 chicken thighs, skin removed
2 medium onions, thinly sliced
2 large cloves garlic, minced
1 (17 ounce) can plum tomatoes, with liquid, coarsely chopped
$1/4$ teaspoon oregano
$1/2$ teaspoon salt
black pepper, to taste
$1/2$ pound feta cheese, sliced
6 ounces spinach noodles, cooked and drained

Heat oil in 10" skillet with lid. Brown chicken pieces over moderate heat, turning them several times. Transfer chicken to platter. Add sliced onions to skillet. Cook onions over moderately low heat, stirring, about 10 minutes. Add garlic and cook for another 5 minutes, or until onions start to brown. Add chopped tomatoes, their liquid and oregano; stir. Place chicken sauce in pan and sprinkle with salt and pepper. Cover the pan, bring to a boil, reduce heat and simmer for 30 minutes. Arrange slices of feta cheese on top of chicken. Cover skillet and cook another 15 minutes, or until chicken is done and cheese is melted. Serve over hot cooked spinach noodles.

"This recipe comes from Jane Brody's "Good Food Book". If serving this to guests, I add Greek olives at the last minute for additional taste."
Julie Blanchard   Western High School, Anaheim, CA

Grilled Balsamic Chicken

Serves 4   ***235 calories, 9 fat grams***

1 (2 $1/2$ to 3 pound) chicken, quartered
$1/4$ cup chicken broth
$1/2$ cup balsamic vinegar
$1/3$ cup scallions, chopped
2 tablespoons dijon mustard
1 tablespoon garlic, minced
1 tablespoon sugar
2 teaspoons worcestershire sauce
1 teaspoon dry mustard
1 teaspoon cracked black pepper

Rinse chicken pieces and pat dry. Arrange chicken in shallow baking dish. In a small bowl, combine remaining ingredients and whisk to blend well. Pour marinade over chicken, cover and refrigerate for at least 24 hours, turning occasionally. Preheat oven to 325 degrees. Prepare grill for cooking. Bring chicken and marinade to room temperature. Bake in oven 30 to 40 minutes. Remove chicken from marinade, reserving marinade. Place chicken on prepared grill and cook 5 to 6 minutes on each side, until tender, basting with the reserved marinade. Serve immediately.

Kathie Baczynski   Mt. Carmel High School, Poway, CA

Healthy Chicken 'n Rice

Serves 6   *435 calories, 9 fat grams*

    nonstick cooking spray
    1 envelope onion soup mix
    1 1/4 cups long grain rice, uncooked
    6 boneless chicken breast halves
    1 can Campbell's Healthy Request Cream of Chicken Soup
    1 can Campbell's Healthy Request Cream of Mushroom Soup
    1 1/2 cups nonfat milk

Spray a 16" x 11" baking pan with nonstick cooking spray. Sprinkle onion soup mix evenly over bottom of pan. Evenly distribute the rice over bottom of pan. Wash chicken breasts; pat dry. Arrange over rice. Mix together soups and milk; pour over chicken and rice. Cover with foil and bake at 350 degrees for 2 hours.

Jill Sweet-Gregory   Santa Paula High School, Santa Paula, CA

Italian Chicken Casserole

Serves 6   *405 calories, 11 fat grams*

    3 skinless chicken breast halves
    1 tablespoon vegetable oil
    1 clove garlic, minced
    1/2 onion, chopped
    2 to 3 zucchini, sliced
    1/2 pound mushrooms, sliced
    1 tomato, cut into 1" pieces
    garlic salt, to taste
    pepper, to taste
    1 1/2 cups spaghetti sauce
    1 cup rice, cooked
    1 cup mozzarella cheese, grated

Cut chicken breasts into bite-sized pieces. Heat oil and add garlic. Add chicken pieces and stir fry until cooked through. Add onions, zucchini and mushrooms and stir fry until just tender, then add tomatoes and cook slightly. Season to taste with garlic salt and pepper. Heat spaghetti sauce in microwave for 1 minute. In a microwave safe casserole dish, stir together cooked rice, chicken mixture and spaghetti sauce. Smooth top and sprinkle with grated cheese. Microwave 6 minutes on high to heat through and melt cheese.

"If you use a nonstick pan, you may not need the vegetable oil to cook the chicken and vegetables. Just put the garlic in with the chicken."

Roberta Marshall   Solano Junior High School, Vallejo, CA

Jamaican Jerk Chicken

Serves 4   *226 calories, 13 fat grams*

$^2/_3$ cup green onions, chopped
3 tablespoons fresh thyme or 1 tablespoon dried
3 tablespoons peanut oil
3 tablespoons soy sauce
2 tablespoons fresh ginger, minced
1 tablespoon garlic, minced
1 habanero chili, seeded, minced or 1 tablespoon serrano chili, minced
1 bay leaf
1 teaspoon coriander
1 teaspoon black pepper
$^1/_3$ teaspoon nutmeg
$^1/_2$ teaspoon allspice
4 large boneless, skinless chicken breast halves

Combine all ingredients (except chicken) in large ziploc bag or covered container, mixing to blend well. Add chicken and marinate in refrigerator several hours or overnight. Grill chicken on covered grill over medium coals 4 to 6 minutes on each side, until just cooked through but still tender and moist.

"I found this recipe in the newspaper, it's been a family favorite."
Cindy Johnson   Orland High School, Orland, CA

Lemon Chicken with Broccoli

Serves 4   *302 calories, 6 fat grams*

4 boneless, skinless chicken breast halves
1 tablespoon cooking oil
2 broccoli crowns, about $^1/_2$ pound
1 teaspoon salt
$^1/_4$ cup sugar
1 $^1/_2$ tablespoons lemon juice
$^3/_4$ cup water
3 tablespoons cornstarch
2 cups steamed rice

Dice chicken into bite sized pieces. Heat oil in skillet and stir fry chicken until done. Break broccoli into flowerets and steam until tender crisp. Add broccoli to chicken. In small saucepan, stir together salt, sugar, lemon juice, water and cornstarch. Heat over medium heat, stirring until sauce thickens. Pour sauce over chicken and broccoli. Heat through and serve over steamed rice.

"Lemon chicken is one of our favorites when we eat Chinese and we really enjoy this lower fat version!"
Kristine Haas   La Habra High School, La Habra, CA

Lemon Sauce Chicken

Serves 4   *150 calories, 1 fat gram*

- nonstick cooking spray
- 4 chicken breast halves
- pinch seasoned salt
- 1 tablespoon wine vinegar
- 1/4 teaspoon lemon peel, grated
- 1 tablespoon lemon juice
- 1/8 teaspoon salt
- 1/8 teaspoon white pepper
- 1 cup chicken broth
- 1/4 cup Parmesan cheese, grated
- 1/2 cup mushrooms, sliced
- lemon wedges and parsley

Spray a large fry pan with nonstick cooking spray. Season chicken breasts with seasoned salt. Over medium heat, cook chicken for about 10 minutes, until brown and fork tender. Remove chicken to oven-proof serving dish. In fry pan, add wine vinegar, lemon peel and lemon juice. Cook 1 minute. Add salt and pepper; pour in chicken broth, stirring constantly to heat, but do not boil. Pour sauce over chicken; sprinkle with Parmesan cheese and mushrooms. With rack about 6" from heat, broil until chicken is lightly browned. Garnish with lemon wedges and parsley.

"This is an excellent lowfat dish which is easily prepared."
Wanda Shelton   Newport Harbor High School, Newport Beach, CA

Lower Fat Chicken Nuggets

Serves 4   *203 calories, 4 fat grams*

- 4 boneless, skinless chicken breast halves
- 1/4 cup Parmesan cheese, grated
- 4 tablespoons lowfat cheddar cheese, grated
- 1/2 cup fine dried bread crumbs
- 1 teaspoon dried thyme
- 1 teaspoon dried basil
- 1/2 teaspoon salt
- 1/8 teaspoon pepper
- dash garlic salt
- 1 can lowfat evaporated milk
- nonstick cooking spray

Cut chicken breasts into 1" squares. Combine cheese, crumbs, thyme, basil, salt, pepper and garlic salt; blend well. Dip chicken pieces into evaporated milk, roll in crumb mixture and arrange on cookie sheet sprayed with nonstick cooking spray. Bake at 375 degrees for 15 to 20 minutes or until tender.

"Also great as an appetizer!"
Lindy Cooper   Sinaloa Junior High School, Simi Valley, CA

Mexican Chicken Lasagna

Serves 12 *253 calories, 6 fat grams*

nonstick cooking spray
$^1/_2$ medium onion, cut into quarters
1 (28 ounce) can whole tomatoes, with juice
$^1/_2$ cup salsa picante or chunky salsa, medium or mild
1 (1 $^1/_4$ ounce) package taco seasoning mix
1 (16 ounce) can black beans, rinsed and drained
1 large egg
1 cup skim milk ricotta cheese
2 cloves garlic, minced
10 uncooked dried lasagna noodles
4 boneless, skinless chicken breast halves, cut into I" cubes
1 (4 ounce) can whole green chiles, cut into thin strips
1 $^1/_2$ cups low fat sharp cheddar, jack or mozzarella cheese (or a combination), shredded

Preheat oven to 350 degrees. Spray 9" x 13" casserole with nonstick cooking spray. To make sauce: in a food processor with metal blade, chop onion. Add tomatoes with juice, salsa and taco seasoning and pulse until tomatoes are in small pieces, 3 or 4 times. Remove to a medium bowl and stir in beans. To make ricotta layer: In a small bowl with a fork, break up egg. Stir in ricotta and garlic. To assemble: Spread 1 cup sauce over the bottom, it will barely cover. Top with 5 noodles, overlapping slightly. Sprinkle with half the chicken, half the chiles, and 2 cups sauce. Spoon ricotta cheese mixture over and spread lightly. Top with half the shredded cheese, remaining noodles, chicken, chiles, sauce and cheese. Bake, uncovered, for 40 minutes, or until noodles are tender when pierced with sharp knife. Cool at least 20 minutes before serving. The casserole will stay warm for up to 1 hour and can be reheated, if desired. (Lasagna may be refrigerated overnight or frozen up to 2 weeks. Bring to room temperature and reheat, covered, at 375 degrees for 20 minutes or in microwave 5 to 10 minutes until heated through.)

"From Entertaining On The Run by Marlene Sorosky Delicious!"
Pat Dallas **Westminster High School, Westminster, CA**

Mozzarella Chicken

Serves 4 *295 calories, 7 fat grams*

1 (26 ounce) jar tomato based pasta sauce
4 boneless, skinless chicken breast halves
4 ounces mozzarella cheese, thinly sliced

Pour sauce into an 8" baking dish. Place chicken in sauce. Cover and bake for 1 hour at 350 degrees. Uncover and place slices of cheese on each breast. Place under broiler and broil for 3 to 4 minutes until cheese is bubbly.

"This dish is good served with pasta or rice."
Cindy Peters **Black Diamond Middle School, Antioch, CA**

Pat's Manicotti

Serves 6   *479 calories, 4 fat grams*

1 pound ground turkey
1/2 onion, chopped
1 teaspoon fresh garlic, crushed
1 package manicotti noodles
16 ounces nonfat cottage cheese
1 pound lowfat mozzarella cheese, shredded
1 jar spaghetti sauce

Cook turkey, onion and garlic, set aside to cool. Boil noodles in salted water for 8 minutes; rinse with cold water and drain. In a bowl, mix together cottage cheese and mozzarella cheese. Combine with turkey mixture. Stuff mixture into cooked noodles. Cover with spaghetti sauce. Place foil over top and bake at 350 degrees for 45 minutes.

"I was trying to cut calories and fat grams in my cooking and came up with this dish. My foods classes love it. It freezes nicely for use later."
Pat Hufnagel   Esperanza High School, Anaheim, CA

Pollo Parmesano

Serves 4   *185 calories, 6 fat grams*

6 tablespoons fine dry bread crumbs
3 tablespoons Parmesan cheese, grated
1 tablespoon parsley, chopped
1/4 teaspoon garlic powder
1/4 teaspoon paprika
1/8 teaspoon thyme
1/8 teaspoon sage
coarsely ground pepper
4 small chicken thighs, skin removed
1/3 cup chicken broth
1/4 cup chicken broth

Preheat oven to 350 degrees. In plastic bag, combine bread crumbs, Parmesan, parsley and seasonings. Place chicken pieces in bag, one at a time and shake bag to coat chicken. Arrange coated chicken in single layer in small, shallow roasting dish. Pour 1/3 cup broth into dish. Bake, uncovered, 30 minutes, basting occasionally. Pour additional 1/4 cup broth over chicken. Cover and bake 10 minutes longer. Remove cover. Baste chicken and bake 5 minutes longer.

"This recipe comes from 'Better Than Fried Chicken' 1987 cookbook by Richard Simmons and Winifred Morice, Home Economist. Really crispy."
Nadya Woelfer   Mayfair High School, Lakewood, CA

Polynesian Chicken

Serves 4   **400 calories, 2 fat grams**

4 (4 ounce) boneless, skinless chicken breast halves
1/3 cup flour
nonstick cooking spray
20 ounces pineapple rings, packed in juice, reserving juice
3/4 cup sugar
1/2 cup apple cider vinegar
2 tablespoons cornstarch
1 cube chicken bouillon
1 teaspoon fresh ginger, grated
1 tablespoon soy sauce
1/2 green bell pepper, sliced in rings
1/2 red bell pepper, sliced in rings

Lightly coat chicken with flour. Brown chicken in frying pan sprayed with nonstick cooking spray. Combine pineapple juice, sugar, vinegar and cornstarch; heat over medium heat until mixture thickens. Add bouillon, ginger and soy sauce. Pour half of the pineapple sauce mixture into 8" square baking dish. Place chicken in sauce, Pour remaining sauce over chicken. Top with pineapple slices and arrange pepper rings on top. Bake at 350 degrees for 1 hour. Serve over hot cooked rice.

"Do not cook chicken until done in fry pan - just brown it. The cooking occurs during the baking."
Diedre Goodnough   Norwalk High School, Norwalk, CA

Roasted Chicken & Vegetables

Serves 4   **405 calories, 13 fat grams**

1 pound red potatoes, unpeeled, cut into wedges
4 large carrots, cut into thirds
1 large onion, cut into 8 wedges
12 cloves garlic, peeled
2 tablespoons olive oil
1 teaspoon salt
3/4 teaspoon dried rosemary leaves, crushed, or 2 tablespoons fresh
1/2 teaspoon pepper
8 chicken thighs, skin removed
1 red pepper, cut into 8 wedges
1 green pepper, cut into 8 wedges
1/2 cup hot water

Preheat oven to 425 degrees. In 15 1/2" x 10 1/2" roasting pan, toss potatoes, carrots, onion and garlic with olive oil, 1/2 teaspoon salt, 1/2 teaspoon rosemary and 1/4 teaspoon black pepper. Cover pan with lid or foil and roast vegetables 20 minutes. Remove from oven; uncover. Add chicken thighs and pepper wedges. Sprinkle with remaining salt, rosemary and black pepper.

Easy Foil-Baked Fish
3 fat grams, see page 102

California Apricot Mixed Grill
6 fat grams, see page 80

Pizza di Napoli
8 fat grams, see page 116

Roast uncovered 25 minutes, stirring vegetable and chicken occasionally to brown evenly. Roast 25 minutes longer, or until vegetables are golden and juices run clear when chicken is pierced. Remove chicken and vegetables to platter; keep warm. Add 1/2 cup hot water to roasting pan, stirring to loosen brown bits from bottom of pan. Spoon sauce over chicken and vegetables to serve.

"Delicious one pan meal completely cooked in the oven. Tarragon may be substituted for the rosemary."
Linda Hsieh   Rowland High School, Rowland Heights, CA

Southwestern Chicken Stir Fry

Serves 4   *150 calories, 4 fat grams*

    2 tablespoons lime juice
    2 teaspoons chili powder
    1 pound boneless, skinless chicken breast halves, cut into 1/2" strips
    nonstick cooking spray
    1 small zucchini, thinly sliced
    1 small yellow summer squash, thinly sliced
    1/3 cup medium picante sauce
    2 tablespoons fresh cilantro, chopped

Mix lime juice and chili powder in medium glass or plastic bowl. Stir in chicken pieces. Cover and refrigerate one hour. Spray 12" nonstick skillet or wok with nonstick cooking spray; heat over medium-high heat. Add chicken and marinade; stir fry about 5 minutes or until chicken is no longer pink in center. Remove chicken from skillet. Spray skillet with nonstick cooking spray again; heat over medium-high heat. Add zucchini and summer squash; stir fry about 4 minutes or until tender crisp. Stir in chicken, picante sauce and cilantro.
April Berry   Temecula Valley High School, Temecula, CA

Speedy Spaghetti Casserole

Serves 3   *251 calories, 8 fat grams*

    1/2 pound ground turkey
    1/4 cup onion, chopped
    3/4 cup spaghetti, broken into 1" pieces
    1 (16 ounce) can tomatoes
    1 teaspoon garlic salt
    1/2 teaspoon oregano
    2 tablespoons ripe olives
    2 tablespoons Parmesan cheese
    1 tablespoon fresh parsley, chopped or 1/2 teaspoon dried parsley

Crumble turkey into ovenproof skillet or skillet that has an ovenproof handle. Add onion and spaghetti and saute over medium heat, stirring constantly for 5 minutes. Add tomatoes, garlic salt and oregano. Bring to boil;

97

then simmer, stirring often for 10 to 20 minutes. Stir in 3/4 of the olives and cheese. Sprinkle parsley and remaining olives and cheese on top. Cover and heat 5 minutes to melt cheese. Transfer skillet to oven and bake at 400 degrees for 20 to 30 minutes.

Ginny Clark   Sonora High School, Sonora, CA

Summer Lime Chicken Breasts

Makes 4   *280 calories, 12 fat grams*

4 skinless chicken breast halves
3 tablespoons olive oil
3 limes, juiced
4 cloves garlic, peeled and minced
3 tablespoons cilantro, chopped
$1/2$ teaspoon salt
$1/2$ teaspoon black pepper
red and yellow bell peppers, roasted

Trim fat from chicken breasts and cut out middle tendon. Pound between waxed paper to flatten slightly. Combine olive oil, lime juice, garlic, 2 tablespoons cilantro, salt and pepper in bowl. Pour over chicken and marinate for 1 hour. Grill or broil the chicken breasts for 2 minutes on each side. Put on platter. Sprinkle with cilantro, serve with roasted red and yellow peppers.

Carolyn McBride   Arcadia High School, Arcadia, CA

Swiss Chicken Rolls

Serves 4   *223 calories, 7 fat grams*

2 thin slices Swiss cheese, reduced fat (about 2 ounces)
4 boneless, skinless chicken breast halves
2 tablespoons flour
$1/2$ teaspoon black pepper
1 tablespoon butter or margarine, reduced fat
$3/4$ cup chicken broth, reduced sodium
fresh parsley, for garnish

Cut each cheese slice in half; place 1 half on top of each chicken breast half. Starting with short end, tightly roll up jelly-roll style. Tie securely with string or use toothpick to hold. On waxed paper, combine flour and pepper; mix well. Add chicken breast rolls; toss gently to coat. In large nonstick skillet, melt butter over medium heat. Add chicken and saute, turning frequently until golden, about 3 minutes. Add broth to skillet. Increase heat and bring to a boil. Reduce heat to medium-low; simmer until chicken is cooked through and sauce is slightly thickened, about 10 to 12 minutes. Place on serving plate; remove string. Garnish with fresh parsley.

"Delicious with fluffy rice. Can be made ahead and heated in the oven."
Shirley Marshman   West Middle School, Downey, CA

Tex Mex Bake

Serves 6   *365 calories, 6 fat grams*

8 ounces thin mostaccioli, uncooked
nonstick cooking spray
1 pound ground turkey breast
1 (10 ounce) package frozen corn, thawed, drained
2/3 cup medium or mild salsa
16 ounces lowfat cottage cheese
1 egg
1 tablespoon cilantro, minced
1/2 teaspoon ground white pepper
1/4 teaspoon ground cumin
1/2 cup Monterey jack cheese, shredded

Preheat oven to 350 degrees. Cook pasta according to package directions, omitting salt. Drain and rinse well; set aside. Spray large nonstick skillet with nonstick cooking spray. Add turkey; cook over high heat until no longer pink, about 5 minutes. Stir in corn and salsa. Remove from heat. Combine cottage cheese, egg, cilantro, white pepper and cumin in small bowl. Spoon 1/2 turkey mixture into bottom of 11" x 8" baking dish. Top with pasta. Spoon cottage cheese mixture over pasta. Top with remaining turkey mixture. Sprinkle with shredded cheese. Bake 25 to 30 minutes, or until heated through.

Leilani Neiner   Fontana High School, Fontana, CA

Thai Pasta With Chicken

Serves 4   *394 calories, 7 fat grams*

3/4 cup reduced sodium chicken broth
1/4 cup seasoned rice vinegar
2 tablespoons reduced sodium soy sauce
1 tablespoon fresh ginger, minced
1 tablespoon garlic, minced
1/4 teaspoon crushed red pepper
3/4 pound fresh or dried linguine
1/2 pound cooked chicken, cut into thin strips
1/3 cup cilantro, minced
2 tablespoons lime juice
2 tablespoons dry roasted peanuts, chopped

Mix together broth, vinegar, soy sauce, ginger, garlic and crushed red pepper in a 2 or 3 quart pan. Cover and bring mixture to a simmer, stirring occasionally, over medium high heat. Prepare linguine according to package directions; drain well. Mix pasta with broth mixture, chicken, cilantro and lime juice. Transfer to a serving bowl or individual plates. Sprinkle with peanuts.

"Great recipe from Sunset magazine."
Carol O'Keefe   Canyon High School, Anaheim Hills, CA

Turkey Meatballs

Serves 6　　　　　　　　*132 calories, 7 fat grams*

Meatballs:
1 pound ground turkey
1/4 cup onion, chopped
1 1/2 teaspoons oregano
1/2 teaspoons mint
1/2 teaspoons parsley
1/2 teaspoons lemon pepper
1 clove garlic, minced
1 teaspoon lemon juice
nonstick cooking spray

Sauce:
1/2 cup nonfat sour cream
1/2 medium cucumber,
　　peeled and finely chopped
1 1/2 teaspoons lemon juice
1/8 teaspoon black pepper

Combine ground turkey, onion, spices, garlic and lemon juice. Shape into balls. Cook in a nonstick skillet sprayed with nonstick cooking spray. Cook 8 to 10 minutes or until browned and no longer pink inside. In a bowl, combine sauce ingredients. Serve meatballs with sauce for dipping.

April Rosendahl　　　　　　　**Chino High School, Chino, CA**

Turkey Tettrazini

Serves 6　　　　　　　　*392 calories, 5 fat grams*

1 cup cooked turkey breast , cut up
16 ounces spaghetti, cooked
1 can Healthy Request Cream of Mushroom Soup
1 cup nonfat milk
1 teaspoon garlic powder
1/2 cup Parmesan cheese, grated

Stir together turkey breast, spaghetti, soup, milk and garlic powder until well mixed. If mixture seems too thick, add 1/2 cup more nonfat milk. Pour into a 9" x 13" oblong pan, sprinkle with Parmesan cheese and bake at 350 degrees for 45 minutes.

Pam Fecchino　　　　　**Cimarron-Memorial High School, Las Vegas, NV**

Zesty Turkey Chili

Serves 6　　　　　　　　*266 calories, 8 fat grams*

nonstick cooking spray
1 pound ground turkey
1/2 cup onion, chopped
2 (15 ounce) cans Mexican-style stewed tomatoes
1 (20 ounce) can pinto beans
1/2 to 2/3 cup salsa (to taste)
1 tablespoon cumin
1 1/2 tablespoons chili powder
1/4 teaspoon black pepper

In a skillet that has been sprayed with nonstick cooking spray, brown ground turkey; drain liquid. Lightly saute onion with turkey until tender. Add remaining ingredients and bring to a boil, then simmer 15 to 20 minutes.

"My UCLA daughter and her roommates say this is a great main dish to serve during the football season while watching the Bruins beat USC!"
Beth Swift   Buena Park High School, Buena Park, CA

Brazilian Baked Fish

Serves 6   *153 calories, 8 fat grams*

1 1/2 teaspoons olive oil
1/2 cup onion, chopped
1/2 cup pimento-stuffed olives, coarsely chopped
1/2 cup red bell pepper, coarsely chopped
3 tablespoons cilantro leaves, chopped
1/3 cup orange juice
2 tablespoons lemon juice
salt and pepper, to taste
1 1/2 pounds cod fillets

Preheat oven to 400 degrees. Heat olive oil over low heat. Saute onion 5 minutes. Add chopped olives, bell pepper, cilantro, juices and salt and pepper. Cut fish into serving pieces. Arrange in greased baking dish and top with sauce. Bake at 400 degrees for 12 to 15 minutes. Serve with juice spooned over the top.
Nancy Bohte   South Pasadena High School, South Pasadena, CA

Creamy Seafood Linguine

Serves 4   *425 calories, 6 fat grams*

8 ounces linguine
nonstick cooking spray, olive oil flavored
1 tablespoon olive oil
1/2 cup onion, finely chopped
5 cloves garlic, minced
3 tablespoons dry white wine
1 tablespoon cornstarch
1 cup evaporated skim milk
1/2 teaspoon ground coriander
8 ounces large shrimp, peeled and deveined
8 ounces bay scallops
3 tablespoons fresh parsley, shipped
1/2 teaspoon salt
1/8 teaspoon ground black pepper

Cook pasta according to package directions; drain and set aside. If necessary, cover to keep warm. Meanwhile, lightly spray a large skillet with olive oil flavored nonstick cooking spray. Add oil and heat over medium-high heat. Add onions and garlic. Cook and stir about 5 minutes or until onions are golden brown. In a small custard cup, stir together wine and cornstarch until smooth. Stir the wine mixture and milk into the onion mixture. Bring the mixture to a simmer over medium heat, stirring constantly. Reduce heat. Stir in coriander and cook for 1 minute. Then add shrimp and scallops. Return to a simmer. Simmer, uncovered, for 3 to 5 minutes, or until shrimp turns pink and scallops are opaque. Stir in parsley, salt and pepper. Serve on top of hot pasta.

Jill Burnham   Bloomington High School, Bloomington, CA

Elegant Tuna and Eggplant Mozzarella

Serves 4   *211 calories, 6 fat grams*

- 1 (1 pound) eggplant
- 1 (7 ounce) can tuna, packed in water
- 3 large tomatoes, seeded and chopped
- 1 small onion, chopped
- 1 medium green pepper, seeded and chopped
- 1 clove garlic, minced
- 2 cups mushrooms
- 1 teaspoon oregano, crumbled
- 1/4 teaspoon rosemary, crumbled
- 1/4 teaspoon salt
- 1 cup part-skim mozzarella cheese, shredded
- 1 tablespoon Parmesan cheese, grated
- 1 tablespoon parsley, chopped

Slice eggplant crosswise in 1/4" thick slices. Steam until tender, 20 to 25 minutes. Arrange in 2 quart shallow casserole dish. Arrange tuna over eggplant. In skillet, combine tomatoes, onion, green pepper, garlic, mushrooms, oregano, rosemary and salt. Cover and simmer 20 minutes. Spoon sauce evenly over tuna and eggplant. Top evenly with mozzarella cheese, then Parmesan cheese. Bake at 350 degrees for 20 minutes. Sprinkle with parsley.

Darlene Brown   Golden Valley Middle School, San Bernardino, CA

Fish In Foil

Serves 6   *170 calories, 3 fat grams*

- 2 pounds fish fillets, such as orange roughy, halibut, flounder, pollock
- 2 cups frozen corn, broccoli, sweet red pepper combination, thawed
- 4 teaspoons lemon herb seasoning
- 2 teaspoons olive oil

Arrange each fillet on an 18" x 12" piece of heavy-duty aluminum foil. Spoon approximately 1/2 cup vegetable mixture onto each fillet. Sprinkle each with 1 teaspoon seasoning and drizzle each with oil. Fold foil around fillets; crimping and sealing edges securely. Transfer to a baking sheet. Bake at 450 degrees for about 15 minutes or until fish flakes easily when tested with fork.

National Fisheries Institute

Fish Tacos

Serves 4   *184 calories, 5 fat grams*

  nonstick cooking spray
  2 tablespoons lemon juice
  $1/8$ teaspoon chili powder
  2 tablespoons cilantro, chopped
  1 (14 ounce) can chicken broth
  $1/2$ pound white fish fillets
  4 corn tortillas
  Garnishes:
  cabbage, shredded
  cilantro, chopped
  yogurt, plain
  salsa
  tomato, chopped
  lime slices

Spray pan with nonstick cooking spray; bring lemon juice, chili powder, cilantro and chicken broth to a boil. Add fish fillets and simmer for 7 to 10 minutes, until fish flakes when tested with fork; drain. While fish is cooking, warm tortillas in microwave oven or on range top. Fill each tortilla with 2 ounces fish and desired garnish.

"Even family members who "hate fish" ask for seconds."
Sue Walters   **Morse High School, San Diego, CA**

Garlicky Shrimp With Salsa

Serves 4   *186 calories, 7 fat grams*

  1 medium onion, cut into $1/2$" wedges
  3 cloves garlic, minced
  1 tablespoon olive oil
  1 (14.5 ounce) can tomatoes, peeled and diced
  2 cups Pace picante sauce
  1 teaspoon thyme leaves
  1 teaspoon ground coriander
  $1/2$ teaspoon salt
  1 pound large shrimp, shelled
  1 large green pepper, cut into strips
  1 tablespoon lemon juice
  $1/4$ cup ripe olives, sliced
  lemon wedges (optional)

Cook onion and garlic in oil over medium-high heat 2 minutes. Add tomatoes, picante sauce, thyme, coriander and salt. Bring to a boil. Reduce heat. Cover, simmer 5 minutes. Stir in shrimp and green pepper; cook, uncovered, until shrimp is cooked and peppers are tender, 5 - 6 minutes. Stir in lemon juice. Sprinkle with olives. Garnish with lemon wedges. Serve over rice or pasta if desired.

"Add 100 calories per 1/2 cup serving when serving over rice."
Pat Curtis   Ensign Intermediate School, Newport Beach, CA

Halibut with Garlic & Mushrooms

Serves 4   *173 calories, 6 fat grams*

5 cloves garlic, unpeeled
3/4 cup chicken stock, defatted
juice of 1 lemon
1/4 teaspoon dried thyme
4 halibut fillets, 1/2" thick
1 tablespoon wine vinegar
1 tablespoon water
2 shallots, minced
1 tablespoon olive oil
1 cup mushrooms, sliced
1/8 teaspoon black pepper

Place 3 cloves garlic in a custard cup and roast at 400 degrees for 15 minutes, or until soft. While garlic is baking, peel and crush remaining 2 cloves garlic. Place in a large pot. Add the chicken stock, lemon juice and thyme. Bring to a boil. Place halibut on a steamer rack and set in the pan. Cover and steam for 7 to 10 minutes, or until cooked through. Remove garlic from oven. Peel, chop and place in a medium bowl. Add vinegar, water and shallots. Whisk in oil. Add mushrooms and pepper. Set aside. Remove halibut from the pan and serve with the mushroom mixture.

"I served this one day at lunch for my department, and it was a big hit."
Diane Castro   Temecula Valley High School, Temecula, CA

Lemon-Ginger Salmon

Serves 2   *233 calories, 9 fat grams*

2 tablespoons teriyaki sauce
2 teaspoons lemon juice
1 small piece ginger root, grated (about 3")
2 (5 ounce) salmon fillets or steaks
2 green onions, sliced
lemon wedges, for garnish

Combine teriyaki sauce, lemon juice, grated ginger root and green onions. Pour over salmon and marinate at least 1 hour in refrigerator. Grill salmon over hot coals or broil, basting with marinade, turning once. Cook 6 - 8 minutes per side, or until fish flakes when tested with fork. Garnish with lemons and serve.

"This is a great recipe for company - delicious and very easy!"
Wendy Johnson   Temecula Valley High School, Temecula, CA

Linguine with Clam Sauce Florentine

Serves 6   *347 calories, 18 fat grams*

1 (10 ounce) package frozen spinach, chopped
2 (10 ounce) cans whole baby clams
1/4 cup olive oil
4 tablespoons butter
1 small onion, minced
1 small garlic clove, minced
1/4 teaspoon salt
1 (16 ounce) package linguine

In medium bowl, place frozen spinach; cover with boiling water and let stand 10 minutes; separate spinach; drain. Drain clams, reserving liquid. Heat oil and butter in 2 quart pan over medium heat; cook onion and garlic until tender. Add salt and clam liquid; heat to boiling, reduce heat to low, cover and simmer 10 minutes. Add clams and spinach. Heat through. Prepare linguine according to package. Add to sauce, toss and heat through. Serve immediately.

"This is a great, quick recipe to make for company."
Deanna Potts   Marina High School, Huntington Beach, CA

Oven Fried Fish

Serves 4   *166 calories, 2 fat grams*

2 cups fat free crackers
1/4 teaspoon dry mustard powder
1 egg white
2 tablespoons nonfat milk
1 pound mild, white flesh fish
lemon wedges

Preheat oven to 425 degree. Process crackers into fine crumbs; stir in mustard. Beat egg white and milk in a shallow bowl. Spread crumbs on a plate. Dip fish in egg mixture, then coat with crumbs on all surfaces. Place on baking sheet and bake about 15 minutes, until fish is crispy and flakes with a fork. Serve with lemon wedges.

"Quick, easy and lowfat."
Janet Worland   Yermo Elementary, Yermo, CA

Parmesan Fish Fillets

Serves 4   *179 calories, 4 fat grams*

4 fresh or frozen fish fillets (totaling 1 pound)
1 egg white, beaten
2 tablespoons water
1/2 cup sodium-reduced wheat wafers, finely crushed
3 tablespoons Parmesan cheese, grated
2 tablespoons parsley, finely snipped
nonstick cooking spray

105

Thaw fish, if frozen. Pat dry with a paper towel. In a small mixing bowl, stir together egg white and water. In another mixing bowl, stir together crushed wafers, Parmesan cheese and snipped parsley. Dip fish into egg white mixture, then into Parmesan mixture to coat. Spray large skillet with nonstick coating. Preheat skillet on medium-high heat. Cook crumb-coated fish in hot skillet for 6 - 8 minutes or until fish flakes with a fork, turning once.

Sue Campbell   Chico Junior High School, Chico, CA

Pasta Alfredo with Smoked Salmon

Serves 6   *357 calories, 8 fat grams*

1 tablespoon reduced calorie margarine
1/4 cup green onion, chopped
2 cloves garlic, minced
1 tablespoon all purpose flour
1 (12 ounce) can evaporated skim milk
2 tablespoons fresh basil, chopped
1/2 cup each Parmesan and Romano cheese, grated
1/2 cup smoked salmon, shredded (about 1/4 pound)
1 (12 ounce) bag mostaccioli, cooked

Melt margarine in saucepan over medium heat; add green onion and garlic and saute 2 minutes. Add flour and stir well. Gradually add milk. Bring to boil, stirring constantly. Reduce heat to medium-low and cook 3 minutes, stirring constantly until slightly thickened (maintain low heat so sauce won't burn). Remove from heat and stir in basil, cheeses and salmon. Combine the sauce with mostaccioli in a large bowl; toss well. Serve immediately.

Angela Croce   Mira Mesa High School, San Diego, CA

Salmon Steak with Lemon-Mustard Sauce

Serves 4   *164 calories, 6 fat grams*

1 teaspoon paprika
1/8 teaspoon garlic powder
2 tablespoons nonfat mayonnaise
2 tablespoons fresh lemon juice
1 teaspoon dijon mustard
1 teaspoon coarse ground black pepper
4 (4 ounce) salmon steaks
nonstick cooking spray
8 lemon wedges, for garnish
parsley, for garnish

Combine first 5 ingredients in small bowl. Blend well and set aside. Sprinkle pepper evenly over both sides of salmon. Place salmon on a broiler rack that has been sprayed with nonstick cooking spray. Broil 2 1/2 minutes on each side or until fish flakes easily. Place on serving plates, spoon mayonnaise mixture over salmon. Serve with lemon wedges and garnish with parsley.

Nan Paul   Grant Middle School, Escondido, CA

Shrimp Creole

Serves 4 - 6   *137 calories, 2 fat grams*

2 medium onions, sliced
1/4 cup green pepper, chopped
6 mushrooms, sliced
1/2 teaspoon salt
1/4 teaspoon paprika
1/4 teaspoon sage
1/8 teaspoon pepper
1/4 teaspoon liquid sweetener
1/2 cup tomato sauce
1 1/2 cups canned tomatoes, drained
2 (5 ounce) cans shrimp
1/4 teaspoon curry powder

Simmer together onions, green pepper, mushrooms, salt, paprika, sage, pepper and sweetener in tomato sauce until tender. Add tomatoes, shrimp and curry powder; heat. Serve hot.

"Very satisfying on a cool evening and low in calories!"
Sharron Maurice   **Blythe Middle School, Blythe, CA**

Tuna Sandwich Spread

Serves 2   *159 calories, 1 fat gram*

1 (6.5 ounce) can light tuna, packed in water, drained
1/4 cup celery, finely chopped
1/4 cup red onion, finely chopped
2 tablespoons parsley, finely chopped
1/3 cup plain nonfat yogurt
1/2 tablespoon honey
1 teaspoon lemon juice
1 tablespoon prepared mustard, spicy or dijon

Flake fish with fork in a medium bowl; add chopped vegetables. In another bowl, stir together yogurt, honey, lemon juice and mustard. Pour dressing over fish and stir until well moistened.

"When I'm trying to lose weight, this is one of my favorite recipes. It's quick, easy and my family likes it. Unless you tell, most people can't tell the difference between yogurt and mayonnaise. You save 244 calories! A typical recipe has 383 calories per serving. This recipe comes from "Cooking Without Fat"."
Beth Kolberg-Bentle   **Rancho High School, No. Las Vegas, NV**

Meatless Main Dishes

Angel Hair Pasta With Tomato And Basil

Serves 2   *340 calories, 5 fat grams*

4 ounces angel hair pasta, cooked and drained
1 teaspoon olive oil
2 cloves garlic, crushed
$1/2$ cup dry white wine
2 tablespoons lemon juice, freshly squeezed
$1/2$ cup tomato sauce
1 cup Roma tomatoes, chopped
$1/4$ cup fresh basil, chopped
2 tablespoons Parmesan cheese, freshly grated
black pepper, freshly ground, to taste

Bring a large pot of water to boil over high heat and maintain at a boil. Add angel hair pasta and cook according to package directions. Put olive oil and garlic in saute pan and cook over medium heat just until garlic begins to brown. Remove saute pan from heat and pour in wine; return to heat. Cook for another 1 to 2 minutes, until wine has been reduced by half. Stir in lemon juice and tomato sauce and reduce again. Add chopped tomato, basil, Parmesan cheese and black pepper. Drain pasta and toss with sauce. Serve immediately.

"This recipe can be doubled. Add fresh mushrooms while sauteing the garlic for a variation. Delicious and low cal."
Armida Gordon   Fountain Valley High School, Fountain Valley, CA

Angel Hair Tomato Sauce

Serves 8   *286 calories, 5 fat grams*

    2 tablespoons olive oil
    2 cloves garlic, minced
    3 pounds Roma tomatoes, chopped
    2 to 3 fresh basil leaves
    1 teaspoon salt
    3 tablespoons Parmesan cheese, grated
    1/4 teaspoon ground pepper, freshly ground
    1 pound angel hair pasta

In large skillet, heat olive oil; stir fry garlic 1 minute, do not brown. Add tomatoes, basil, salt and pepper and cook for 2 minutes, stirring often. Keep warm. Prepare pasta according to package directions; drain. Toss sauce with hot cooked pasta. Serve with Parmesan cheese

"A great, quick and wonderful light dinner. Serve with French bread and a salad."
Beverly Ranger   Carpinteria High School, Carpinteria, CA

Cheesy Vegetable Shells

Serves 5   *260 calories, 5 fat grams*

    nonstick cooking spray
    15 jumbo pasta shells, uncooked
    15 ounces chunky tomato sauce
    1 cup tomato sauce
    1 teaspoon olive oil
    1/2 cup carrots, shredded
    1/2 cup summer squash , shredded
    1/2 cup zucchini, shredded
    2 ounces or 1/2 cup mushrooms, sliced
    1/4 cup green onion, sliced
    1 clove garlic, finely chopped
    2 cups nonfat or lowfat ricotta cheese
    1/4 cup Parmesan cheese, grated
    1/4 cup cholesterol-free egg product or 2 egg whites, slightly beaten
    2 teaspoons dried basil
    1/2 cup reduced fat mozzarella cheese, shredded

Heat oven to 350 degrees. Spray 11" x 7" baking dish with nonstick cooking spray. Cook and drain pasta shells according to package directions; set aside. Mix tomato sauces. Spoon half of the tomato sauce into baking dish. Heat oil in 10" skillet over medium-high heat. Cook carrot, squash, zucchini, mushrooms, onion and garlic in oil, stirring frequently until vegetables are crisp tender. Stir in remaining ingredients, except tomato sauce. Fill shells with vegetable/cheese mixture. Place in baking dish. Spoon remaining tomato sauce over shells. Cover and bake 40 to 45 minutes or until hot and bubbly.

109

Sprinkle with shredded Parmesan cheese, if desired.

"I think this is a good lowfat lasagna substitute. You could use a variety of different vegetables in it."
Anita Cornwall   **Cimarron-Memorial High School, Las Vegas, NV**

Chili "Non Carne"

Serves 8   *157 calories, 5 fat grams*

- 3/4 cup onion, chopped
- 2 cloves garlic, minced
- 3 tablespoons olive oil
- 2 tablespoons chili powder
- 1/4 teaspoon basil
- 1/4 teaspoon oregano
- 1/4 teaspoon cumin
- 2 cups zucchini, finely chopped
- 1 cup carrot, finely chopped
- 1 (28 ounce) can tomatoes, chopped
- 1 (14 1/2 ounce) can tomatoes, drained and chopped
- 1 (15 ounce) can kidney beans, undrained
- 2 (15 ounce) cans kidney beans, thoroughly drained and rinsed
- Garnishes: chopped onion, chopped tomatoes, shredded lettuce, chopped green pepper

In a large pot, saute onion and garlic in olive oil until soft. Mix in chili powder, basil, oregano and cumin. Stir in zucchini and carrots until well blended. Cook for about 1 minute over low heat, stirring occasionally. Stir in all chopped tomatoes and all kidney beans. Bring to a boil; reduce heat and simmer 30 to 45 minutes, or until thick. Top with desired garnish.

"Chili is traditionally made with beef. You will not miss the beef in this recipe. Beans, such as kidney beans have been shown to be effective in lowering blood cholesterol."
Vicki Giannetti   **Foothill High School, Sacramento, CA**

Fettuccine Alfredo

Serves 6   *511 calories, 13 fat grams*

- 1 tablespoon + 1 1/2 teaspoons margarine
- 3 small cloves garlic, minced
- 1 tablespoon + 1 1/2 teaspoons all-purpose flour
- 2 cups skim milk
- 3 tablespoons light process cream cheese product
- 2 cups fresh Parmesan cheese, grated
- 6 cups hot cooked fettuccine (3/4 of 12 ounce box), cooked without salt or fat
- 1 tablespoon fresh parsley or basil, chopped
- freshly ground pepper

Melt margarine in saucepan over medium heat. Add garlic, saute 1 minute. Stir in flour. Gradually add milk, stirring with a wire whisk until blended. Cook 10 minutes or until thickened and bubbly, stirring constantly. Stir in cream cheese; cook 2 minutes. Add 1 1/2 cups Parmesan cheese, stirring constantly until it melts. Pour over hot cooked fettuccine; toss well to coats. Top with remaining 1/2 cup Parmesan cheese, fresh parsley or basil and pepper.

Jill Marsh   Warren High School, Downey, CA

Garden Pasta

Serves 8   *250 calories, 3 fat grams*

    5 medium tomatoes, chopped
    2 stalks celery, chopped
    2 medium carrots, chopped
    1 medium onion, chopped
    1 packet Equal (sugar substitute)
    1 teaspoon basil
    $1/4$ teaspoon garlic powder
    $1/2$ teaspoon salt
    $1/2$ teaspoon pepper
    $1/2$ teaspoon oregano
    1 tablespoon olive oil
    1 pound spaghetti

Put all vegetables in pot and and cover tightly. Cook over medium heat, stirring occasionally, for 10 minutes. Add the seasonings. Recover the pot and cook over medium-low heat for 5 minutes. Add the oil and simmer for 30 minutes, or until the carrots are tender. Cook spaghetti according to package directions, drain. Toss with sauce and serve.

"From a hospital nutritionist, suitable for lowfat diabetic diets!"
Vanessa Van Assen   Fort Bragg High School, Fort Bragg, CA

Light & **Delicious**

Grilled Vegetable Sandwich

Serves 6 **258 calories, 3 fat grams**

Dressing:
1 cup plain nonfat yogurt
3 tablespoons dijon mustard
pepper, freshly ground, to taste
2 tablespoons nonfat cottage cheese
1/8 teaspoon tabasco sauce
2 tablespoons shallots, minced (1 small shallot)
1 clove garlic, peeled and minced
1 teaspoon lemon juice, freshly squeezed
Sandwich filling:
1 medium yellow squash, trimmed and cut into 1/4" rounds
1 medium zucchini, trimmed and cut into 1/4" rounds
1 red onion, trimmed and cut into 1/4" rounds
3 teaspoons Italian seasoning
1/8 teaspoon cayenne pepper
nonstick cooking spray
2 red bell peppers, roasted
2 Boboli pizza breads
1 large tomato, cored and sliced
black pepper, freshly ground, to taste
2 tablespoons jalapeno pepper, chopped (1 large pepper)
8 fresh basil leaves
8 arugula leaves

Preheat broiler. Put all dressing ingredients in a a blender and mix at low speed until smooth; set aside. Arrange yellow squash, zucchini and onion in a single layer on cookie sheet. Sprinkle with Italian seasoning and cayenne pepper and spray with nonstick cooking spray to coat lightly. Broil vegetables for about 5 minutes, until brown; turn rounds over and brown the other side. Remove cookie sheet from broiler, remove vegetables to platter. Quarter roasted peppers. Cut each Boboli pizza bread in half lengthwise and place on broiler rack. Toast about 2 minutes on each side; remove from broiler. Arrange half the tomato slices on bottom of each crust. Dust with black pepper and jalapeno peppers. Place basil and arugula leaves and roasted peppers on top of tomatoes. Layer slices of squash, zucchini and onion on top. Coat the inside of the remaining halves of each Boboli pizza bread with dressing and place on top of vegetables. Cut each into three large sandwiches **Note:** To roast peppers slice in half lengthwise, core and remove seeds. Put sliced peppers on rack of preheated broiler, cut side down. Broil for about 5 minutes, until skin blisters. Transfer roasted peppers to tightly sealing plastic bag, close it, and leave for 10 to 15 minutes. When cool, the charred skin can be rubbed easily from peppers and discarded.

"Tasty recipe from "Cooking With Rosie". Use vegetables of your choice."
Luann Goedert Carlsbad High School, Carlsbad, CA

Idaho Chili

Serves 6   *134 calories, 2 fat grams*

1 (32 ounce) can tomato juice
2 cups water
2 medium potatoes, peeled and chopped
1 (15 ounce) can garbanzo beans, undrained
1 cup lentils, rinsed and drained
1 large onion, chopped
2 carrots, cut into 1" julienne strips
2 tablespoons chili powder
2 teaspoons instant beef bouillon granules
1 teaspoon dried basil
$1/2$ teaspoon garlic powder
Optional Toppings: sour cream, tortilla chips, snipped chives

In a single pot, stir together all ingredients except optional items. Bring to a boil and then reduce heat. Simmer, covered, for about 30 minutes or until lentils are tender.

"The finished product will be thick and can be eaten with tortilla chips. It's fast, easy, cheap and nutritious. Compliments of Steve Mitrovich."
Peggy Herndon   **Central Valley High School, Shasta Lake City, CA**

Impossible Spinach-Feta Pie

Serves 6   *200 calories, 10 fat grams*

nonstick cooking spray
1 (10 ounce) package frozen chopped spinach, thawed and drained
$1/3$ cup onion, finely chopped
$1/2$ cup mushrooms, thinly sliced
4 ounces feta cheese, crumbled
1 $1/2$ cups nonfat milk
3 egg whites or $3/4$ cup liquid egg substitute
$3/4$ cup Bisquick baking mix
$1/4$ teaspoon salt (optional)
$1/8$ teaspoon pepper
2 tablespoons Parmesan cheese, grated

Heat oven to 400 degrees. Spray 10" x 1 1/2" pie plate with nonstick cooking spray. Layer spinach, onion and mushrooms in pie plate. Sprinkle with feta cheese. Blend next five ingredients until smooth, 15 seconds in blender or 1 minute with hand beater. Pour over layered vegetables and cheese; sprinkle with Parmesan cheese. Bake for 30 minutes or until knife inserted in center comes out clean. Cool 5 minutes before serving.
Ellen Gordon   **Colton High School, Colton, CA**

Italian Pasta Stir Fry

Serves 6   *186 calories, 4 fat grams*

8 ounces linguine, cooked
1 tablespoon olive oil
2 large cloves garlic, pressed
1 medium zucchini, sliced
1 medium onion, chopped
2 medium tomatoes, peeled and chopped
1/4 cup fresh parsley, minced
1 teaspoon dried oregano
1/8 teaspoon salt
1/8 teaspoon ground black pepper
1/4 cup Parmesan cheese, grated

Cook pasta according to package directions. Keep warm. Heat olive oil; add garlic. Stir fry 15 seconds, add zucchini and onion. Stir fry 2 to 3 minutes, until crisp and tender. Add tomatoes, parsley and seasonings to skillet. Gently stir 1 to 2 minutes, until thoroughly heated. Remove from heat. Stir in warm pasta and Parmesan cheese. Serve immediately.

Astrid Curfman   **Newcomb Academy, Long Beach, CA**

Jeff's Special Meatless Meal

Serves 6   *389 calories, 6 fat grams*

1 large or 2 small bell peppers
2 tablespoons oil
1 medium onion, chopped
1/2 teaspoon thyme
1/2 teaspoon rosemary
1/4 teaspoon dill weed
1/8 teaspoon cayenne pepper
2 cups brown rice, cooked
1 (16 ounce) can tomatoes, cut up
1 (16 ounce) can kidney beans, drained

Remove seeds and membrane from peppers, cut into 1/2" square pieces. In 8" fry pan, heat oil; add onion and saute over medium heat until translucent. Add spices and bell pepper. Continue to saute until onions begin to brown. Reduce heat to medium. Add tomatoes with juice and beans. Cook 1 to 2 minutes. Add rice and heat through, about 1 to 2 minutes more, stirring to prevent sticking.

"This is a simple recipe to fix. My husband, Jeff, created it. He prefers using mixed peppers and black beans for a colorful dish."
Sally Spieker-Slaughter   **Tehachapi High School, Tehachapi, CA**

Okra Tomato Stew

Serves 6   *85 calories, 5 fat grams*

  2 cloves garlic, minced
  2 tablespoons olive oil
  1 medium onion, chopped
  1 (16 ounce) package frozen okra, cut
  1 (16 ounce) can tomatoes, chopped
  $1/4$ teaspoon cayenne
  1 teaspoon chili powder
  $1/2$ teaspoon salt

In large saucepan, saute garlic in olive oil until tender. Add remaining ingredients and simmer over low heat for 30 to 45 minutes.

"This dish is part of our traditional New Year's dinner of black-eyed peas, mashed potatoes and cornbread. It is a great lowfat meal to start off the New Year!"
Katherine Iverson   Vandenberg Middle School, Lompoc, CA

Pasta Delight

Serves 8   *215 calories, 1 fat gram*

  8 cups water
  10 chicken bouillon cubes
  $1/2$ teaspoon oregano
  $1/2$ teaspoon garlic powder
  $1/2$ teaspoon onion powder
  $1/2$ teaspoon thyme
  $1/2$ teaspoon black pepper
  1 teaspoon parsley
  1 medium onion, diced
  3 stalks celery, chopped
  1 cup frozen peas
  1 small tomato, diced
  1 (12 ounce) package fideo pasta

Put water, bouillon cubes and seasonings in a large Dutch oven; bring to a boil. Add all vegetables and simmer for 3 minutes. Add broken fideo pasta; boil for 5 minutes. Lower heat and simmer for 10 minutes. **Note:** You can substitute other pasta for fideo. You can also use leftover meat, cut into bite-sized pieces and vegetables of your choice. Experiment!

"Great dish and easy...Enjoy!!!"
Teresa Stahl   Needles High School, Needles, CA

Pepper Pizzas

Serves 4   *275 calories, 11 fat grams*

4 (6 - 7") flour tortillas
4 medium peppers, cut into strips
2 medium onions, sliced
2 cloves garlic, minced
1 teaspoon oregano
1 teaspoon salt
1/4 teaspoon coarse black pepper
1/2 pound mushrooms, sliced
1/2 cup spaghetti or pizza sauce
4 ounces mozzarella cheese, shredded

On microwave-cooking rack, place 2 tortillas, cover with paper towel, then top with remaining 2 tortillas. Cook on high 3 1/2 to 4 1/2 minutes until tortillas are puffy and crisp; set aside. In 3 quart casserole, cook peppers and next 5 ingredients; covered, on high 10 to 12 minutes until tender-crisp; stirring halfway through cooking. Stir in mushrooms; cook, covered, 3 to 4 minutes until vegetables are tender. In a cup, heat spaghetti sauce on high 1 to 1 1/2 minutes; Spread some sauce on each tortilla; top with vegetable mixture; sprinkle with cheese. On microwave safe platter, cook 4 "pizzas" on high 3 to 4 minutes until cheese melts.

"I love pizza anyway I can get it! This is a nice low calorie treat!"
Laura Bosma   A.B. Miller High School, Fontana, CA

Pizza Di Napoli

Serves 6   *271 calories, 8 fat grams*

3 tablespoons pesto sauce
1 (12") prebaked pizza crust
3 plum tomatoes, sliced
1 (4 ounce) ball Wisconsin Fresh Mozzarella cheese, thinly sliced
1/3 cup pitted ripe olive slivers
1 tablespoon fresh oregano leaves, minced

Spread pesto evenly over crust; top with tomato slices, cheese and olives. Place on cookie sheet or bake directly on oven rack at 450 degrees for 8 minutes or until cheese is melted. Sprinkle with oregano. **Pizza Primavera:** Omit pesto sauce, tomatoes, olives and oregano. Spread crust with 1/4 cup commercial alfredo sauce; top with 1 cup yellow summer squash slices, 1/4 cup thawed frozen peas, 2 ounces thinly sliced prosciutto, julienne cut, and cheese. Bake as directed. Sprinkle with 2 tablespoons slivered fresh basil leaves. **Tri-Pepper Pizza:** Omit pesto sauce, tomatoes and olives. Top crust with 1/2 cup each: yellow, red and orange or green bell pepper strips and 1/4 cup red onion slivers. Dot with 1/2 cup chopped marinated sun dried tomatoes. Top with cubed or diced mozzarella cheese and 1/4 cup grated Wisconsin Asiago cheese. Bake as directed; sprinkle with oregano.

Rice & Bean Stuffed Peppers

Serves 6   *233 calories, 2 fat grams*

- 1/2 cup onion
- 2 teaspoons water
- 1 cup tomato sauce
- 2/3 cup instant rice
- 1/2 teaspoon sugar
- 1/4 teaspoon pepper
- 1/2 teaspoon basil
- 1/2 teaspoon oregano
- 1/4 teaspoon chili powder
- 2 (8 ounce) cans black beans
- 1 cup corn, whole kernel
- 3 green, red or yellow bell peppers
- 1/4 cup lowfat mozzarella cheese, shredded

Saute onion in 2 teaspoons water to soften. Add tomato sauce, rice, sugar and spices and slowly bring to a low boil. Simmer for 5 minutes. Add beans and corn and heat through. Cut peppers in half and parboil 1 - 2 minutes, or until tender; drain. Place on cookie sheet, cut side up. Spoon rice mixture into pepper halves and sprinkle with cheese. Bake at 350 degrees for 20 minutes.

"A colorful main dish that is nutritious and tasty too!"
Toni Purtill   Basic High School, Henderson, NV

Vegetable Lasagna

Serves 6   *258 calories, 4 fat grams*

- 8 ounces lasagna noodles
- 1 medium zucchini, thinly sliced
- 1 1/2 teaspoons olive oil
- 1 medium onion, finely chopped
- 1 garlic clove, minced
- 1 (10 ounce) package frozen broccoli, chopped, thawed and well-drained
- 3/4 cup low-fat ricotta cheese
- 2 tablespoons Parmesan cheese
- 1 tablespoon parsley flakes
- 1/2 teaspoon salt
- 1/4 teaspoon pepper
- 1 1/2 cups tomato sauce
- 2 ounces lowfat mozzarella cheese, grated

Bring a large pot filled with salted water to a boil. Add lasagna noodles and cook 7 to 10 minutes; drain and rinse. Place zucchini in microwave bowl with 3 tablespoons water. Cover with plastic wrap and cook on HIGH for 1 minute. Drain and set aside. In a medium saucepan, heat olive oil; add onion and cook for 3 minutes. Add garlic and cook 1 minute longer. Remove from heat. Add chopped broccoli, ricotta, Parmesan, parsley, salt and pepper; blend well. Fold in cooked zucchini. Spread 2 tablespoons tomato sauce over bottom of a 9" x 9" x 2" baking dish. Arrange a single layer of lasagna noodles over sauce. Spread half of vegetable filling over noodles and spoon 1/3 remaining tomato sauce over filling. Make another layer with half of remaining noodles, all of remaining filling and half of remaining tomato sauce. Top with remaining noodles and sauce. Sprinkle mozzarella cheese evenly over top. Bake at 400 degrees for 30 minutes.

Donna Joaquin   Sequoia Junior High School, Simi Valley, CA

Won't Miss the Meat Pizza

Serves 4   *521 calories, 17 fat grams*

2 teaspoons olive oil
1 medium yellow onion, finely chopped
1 tablespoon garlic, minced
$^1/_4$ teaspoon salt
$^1/_4$ teaspoon pepper
$^1/_2$ green pepper, chopped
4 large mushrooms, sliced
2 zucchini, sliced
1 cup broccoli flowerets
1 $^1/_2$ cups pizza sauce
1 cup mozzarella cheese, shredded
1 14" pizza crust
2 tablespoons Parmesan cheese, grated

Preheat oven to 450 degrees. Heat olive oil over moderate heat in a large skillet. Add onion and garlic, salt and pepper and saute, stirring occasionally, for 5 minutes or until golden brown. Add mushrooms, green pepper, zucchini and broccoli, stirring continuously for 3 minutes, or until mushrooms are tender. Spread pizza dough with pizza sauce. Spread vegetable mixture evenly over sauce. Sprinkle with cheese and top with Parmesan. Bake for 20 minutes.

"A fun way to eat your vegetables! Kids love it!"
Nancie Wilson   Woodland High School, Woodland, CA

Desserts

Angel Food Cake with Frosting

Serves 16   **130 calories, 0 fat grams**

Cake:
1 ¹/₂ cups powdered sugar
1 cup cake flour
1 ¹/₂ cups egg whites (about 12 eggs)
1 ¹/₂ teaspoons cream of tartar
1 cup granulated sugar
1 ¹/₂ teaspoons vanilla
¹/₂ teaspoon almond extract
¹/₄ teaspoon salt

Frosting:
¹/₂ cup granulated sugar
¹/₄ cup light corn syrup
2 tablespoons water
2 egg whites
1 teaspoon vanilla
Food coloring (optional) ¹/₂ cup sugar
¹/₄ cup light corn syrup
2 tablespoons water
2 egg whites
1 teaspoon vanilla
Food coloring (optional)

Move oven rack to lower position. Remove upper rack. Heat oven to 375 degrees. Mix powdered sugar and flour together. In another bowl, beat egg whites with cream of tartar on medium speed until foamy. Beat in granulated sugar on high speed, 2 tablespoons at a time, adding vanilla, almond extract and salt with last addition of sugar. Continue beating until stiff and glossy. Do not underbeat. Sprinkle sugar-flour mixture 1/4 cup at a time over meringue, folding just until sugar-flour mixture disappears. Push batter into ungreased tube pan, 10" x 4". Cut gently through batter to remove air bubbles. Bake 30 to 35 minutes until cracks in cake feel dry and top springs back when touched lightly. Immediately turn pan upside down onto glass bottle. Let hang 2 hours or until cake is completely cool. Remove from pan.

119

While cake is cooling, prepare frosting: mix sugar, corn syrup and water in small saucepan. Cover and heat to rolling boil over medium heat. Uncover and cook, without stirring, to 242 degrees on candy thermometer. Tilt the pan to get accurate reading. (It takes 4 to 9 minutes to reach 242 degrees.) While mixture boils, beat egg whites in medium bowl just until stiff peaks form. Don't overbeat. Pour hot syrup very slowly in thin stream into egg whites, beating constantly on medium speed. Add vanilla. Beat on high speed about 10 minutes, until stiff peaks form. Add a few drops of food coloring, if desired. Frost cake.

Charlotte Runyan   Saddleback High School, Santa Ana, CA

Apple Cake

Serves 12 - 16   *301 calories, 13 fat grams*

nonstick cooking spray
1 $1/4$ cups sugar
1 cup canola oil
$1/2$ cup unsweetened applesauce
$2/3$ cup liquid egg substitute
1 teaspoon vanilla
2 cups unbleached all-purpose flour
1 teaspoon baking soda
$1/2$ teaspoon salt
1 $1/2$ teaspoons cinnamon
3 medium apples, peeled, cored and chopped to make 3 cups
$1/2$ cup walnuts, chopped and toasted

Preheat oven to 350 degrees. Spray a 9" x 13" baking pan with nonstick cooking spray; set aside. In a large bowl, combine sugar, oil, applesauce, egg substitute and vanilla; mix well. In a separate bowl, combine flour, baking soda, salt and cinnamon. Add the flour mixture to the sugar mixture and stir just until combined. Stir in apples and walnuts and pour into prepared pan. Bake 45 to 50 minutes.

"Delicious served warm or at room temperature."
Olga Sarouhan   Edison High School, Huntington Beach, CA

Apple Crisp

Serves 8   *215 calories, 0 fat grams*

6 medium apples, peeled and coarsely chopped
1 tablespoon lemon juice
$3/4$ cup + 2 tablespoons frozen apple juice concentrate, thawed and divided
$3/4$ teaspoon cinnamon
$1/4$ teaspoon ground nutmeg
$1/2$ cup raisins
$1/4$ cup dates, chopped
1 $1/2$ cups fat free granola (without fruit added)

Preheat oven to 350 degrees. In 8" x 11" x 2" ovenproof glass baking dish, stir together apples, lemon juice and 3/4 cup apple juice concentrate, cinnamon, nutmeg, raisins and dates. In food processor, blend together granola and remaining apple juice concentrate for 2 minutes. Top apple mixture and bake for 30 minutes

Ellen Pepin   Moreno Valley High School, Moreno Valley, CA

Banana Macadamia Frozen Lowfat Yogurt

Makes 4 quarts (32 servings)   *145 calories, 4.5 fat grams*

- 6 medium bananas
- 8 tablespoons light corn syrup
- 2 cups sugar
- 4 teaspoons lemon juice
- 4 teaspoons pure vanilla extract
- 2 $\frac{1}{4}$ cups lowfat milk
- 4 cups plain nonfat yogurt
- 1 $\frac{1}{3}$ cups macadamia nuts, chopped (or other nuts of your choice)

In a large mixing bowl, combine bananas, corn syrup, sugar, lemon juice and vanilla. Process in batches in a food processor using a metal blade until bananas are pureed. Combine pureed mixture with milk and yogurt, mixing well. Stir in nuts. Freeze in an ice cream freezer according to directions.

"My son's girlfriend made this for a party. She made it up. We all loved it!"
Deanne Moody   Monte Vista High School, Spring Valley, CA

Bran Cake

Serves 9   *220 calories, 6 fat grams*

- 1 $\frac{1}{2}$ cups flour
- 1 $\frac{1}{2}$ cups bran flake cereal with raisins
- 1 teaspoon baking powder
- $\frac{1}{2}$ teaspoon baking soda
- $\frac{1}{2}$ teaspoon salt
- $\frac{1}{4}$ cup butter or margarine, melted
- 1 egg, slightly beaten
- 1 cup buttermilk
- 2 tablespoons sugar, for topping
- $\frac{1}{2}$ teaspoon cinnamon, for topping

Heat oven to 400 degrees. Grease bottom of 8" square or 9" round cake pan. Lightly spoon flour into measuring cup; level off. In large bowl, combine remaining ingredients, except sugar and cinnamon, and stir until ingredients are moistened. Spread batter in greased pan. Combine cinnamon and sugar; sprinkle over batter. Bake 30 to 40 minutes, test with toothpick. Serve warm.

"Especially good served warm. If you don't have buttermilk, use 1 tablespoon vinegar or lemon juice in 1 cup milk."
Val Herford   Mesa Intermediate School, Palmdale, CA

Breakfast Cookies

Makes 48   *132 calories, 6 fat grams*

- 2 1/4 cups flour
- 2 cups brown sugar, firmly packed
- 1 teaspoon baking powder
- 1/2 teaspoon salt
- 1/2 cup butter or margarine
- 1/2 cup applesauce
- 2 teaspoons vanilla
- 4 egg whites
- 1/4 cup dry milk powder
- 3/4 cup peanut butter
- 2 cups quick-cooking rolled oats, uncooked
- 1/2 cup walnuts, chopped
- 3/4 cup raisins
- nonstick cooking spray
- 1 cup semi-sweet chocolate chips (optional)

Heat oven to 350 degrees. Lightly spoon flour into measuring cup, level it off. In a large bowl, combine flour, brown sugar, baking soda, salt, butter or margarine, applesauce, vanilla and egg whites. Beat at medium speed with an electric mixer until just mixed. Add dry milk powder and peanut butter; continue to blend by hand until mixture is uniform. Stir in oats, nuts, chips and raisins. Drop by rounded tablespoonfuls 2" apart onto cookie sheet sprayed with nonstick cooking spray. Bake for 10 to 12 minutes. Cool for 1 to 2 minutes on cookie sheet; carefully remove and cool on racks. NOTE: Because recipe has been reduced in fat, overmixing batter will make it tough.

"These cookies contain four food groups. One large or two small cookies make a serving."
Diane Heider   Hedrick Middle School, Medford, OR

Cantaloupe Dessert Topping

Makes 3 cups   *27 calories, 0 fat grams*

- Juice from 1/2 orange
- Juice of 1 lime
- 2 tablespoons honey
- 1 medium cantaloupe, seeded, peeled and cubed

Place juices and honey in blender or food processor with blade. Add cantaloupe and blend until smooth. Serve.

"Use as a dip for fruit kabobs or serve over fruit or ice cream."
Amy Tavaglione-Rudolph   Etiwanda High School, Rancho Cucamonga, CA

Caramel Corn

Serves 4   *82 calories, 0 fat grams*

2 tablespoons sugar
2 tablespoons caramel topping
1/2 teaspoon vanilla
4 teaspoons vinegar
4 cups popcorn, popped

In nonstick skillet, heat sugar over very low heat, stirring constantly, until sugar turns brown. Add caramel topping, vanilla and vinegar and continue cooking, stirring vigorously, until all lumps disappear and mixture is bubbly. Pour mixture over popcorn in a heat-proof bowl. Moisten hands with cold water and shape into 8 equal balls. Let cool before serving.

Carmen Leonard   Mission Viejo High School, Mission Viejo, CA

Chewy Brownies

Serves 10   *167 calories, 4 fat grams*

nonstick cooking spray
1 cup flour
1 cup powdered sugar
1/4 cup + 1/2 teaspoon cocoa
1/4 teaspoon baking powder
1 1/2 ounces semi-sweet chocolate, coarsely broken
3 tablespoons margarine (not diet, tub-style)
1/2 cup brown sugar, firmly packed
2 tablespoons corn syrup
1 tablespoon water
2 teaspoons vanilla
2 large egg whites

Preheat oven to 350 degrees. Line an 8" square pan with foil, making sure foil overlaps pan by about 1 1/4" on two ends. Coat foil with nonstick cooking spray; set aside. Measure flour, powdered sugar, cocoa and baking powder into bowl, Place chocolate and margarine in medium saucepan. Stir over lowest heat until chocolate is just melted and smooth. Remove pan from heat and stir in brown sugar, corn syrup, water and vanilla until well blended. Using a wooden spoon, beat egg whites into chocolate mixture. Gently stir in flour mixture just until well blended and smooth. Transfer batter to prepared pan, spreading evenly with rubber spatula. Bake 24 to 28 minutes or until center of top is almost firm when tapped. Let stand 15 minutes. Using overhanging foil as handles, carefully lift brownies from pan and place on foil on cooling rack.

"This recipe was the overwhelming favorite of my Food Science students!"
Mary Rector   Valley High School, Las Vegas, NV

Chocolate Amaretto Cheesecake

Serves 12   *213 calories, 8 fat grams*

6 chocolate wafers, finely crushed
1 1/2 cups light cream cheese
1 cup sugar
1 cup 1% lowfat cottage cheese
1/4 cup + 2 tablespoons unsweetened cocoa powder
1/4 cup all-purpose flour
1/4 cup amaretto liqueur
1 teaspoon vanilla extract
1/4 teaspoon salt
1 egg
2 tablespoons semi-sweet chocolate mini-morsels
3 squares semi-sweet chocolate

Sprinkle chocolate wafers in bottom of 7" springform pan; set aside. In a bowl, add cream cheese and next 7 ingredients; blend until smooth in mixer or food processor. Add egg; mix until well blended. Fold in chocolate morsels. Slowly pour mixture over crumbs in pan. Bake at 300 degrees for 65 to 70 minutes or until cheesecake is set. Let cool in pan on wire rack. Cover and chill at least 8 hours. Remove sides of pan and transfer to serving platter and decorate   with   chocolate   curls,   if   desired. To make chocolate curls: melt 3 squares semi-sweet chocolate. Pour melted chocolate onto wax paper and spread to a 3" wide strip. Let stand until cool but not firm. Pull a vegetable peeler across chocolate and transfer curls to a plate. Store chocolate curls in the freezer.

"You may substitute creme de menthe for the amaretto."
Christine Williams   **Red Bluff Union High School, Red Bluff, CA**

Chocolate Chip Yogurt Cookies

Makes 3 dozen   *90 calories, 4 fat grams*

1/2 cup sugar
1/2 cup brown sugar, firmly packed
1/4 cup margarine or butter, softened
1/4 cup shortening
1/2 cup nonfat yogurt, plain
1 1/2 teaspoons vanilla
1 3/4 cups flour
1/2 teaspoon baking soda
1/2 teaspoon salt
1 cup semi-sweet chocolate chips

Preheat oven to 375 degrees. Beat sugar, brown sugar, margarine or butter and shortening until light and fluffy. Add yogurt and vanilla; blend. Stir in flour, baking soda and salt; stir in chocolate chips. Drop by spoonfuls on ungreased cookie sheet. Bake 8 to 12 minutes.

"This is a chocolate chip cookie recipe remake using yogurt for part of the margarine."
Jeanette Atkinson   Brinley Middle School, Las Vegas, NV

Chocolate Gourmet Delight

Serves 12   *384 calories, 16 fat grams*

- 1/2 cup margarine, softened
- 1 cup flour
- 1 cup walnuts or almonds, chopped
- 8 ounces light whipped topping
- 1 cup powdered sugar
- 1 (8 ounce) fat free cream cheese
- 3 3/4 cups nonfat milk
- 3 small boxes chocolate pudding, sugar-free

Preheat oven to 350 degrees. Mix together margarine, flour and nuts; pat into bottom of 13" x 9" pan. Bake 15 minutes; cool. Blend whipped topping, powdered sugar and cream cheese together and spread on cooled crust. Blend nonfat milk with pudding mix and spread on top of mixture. Top with additional whipped topping and sprinkle with nuts, if desired.

"A favorite. Some of the ingredients make it lower in fat and calories."
Roberta Hawkes   A.B. Miller High School, Fontana, CA

Chocolate Pudding Cake

Serves 12   *168 calories, 2 fat grams*

Cake:
- 1 cup flour
- 1/2 teaspoon salt
- 3/4 cup sugar, divided
- 2 teaspoons baking powder
- 1 1/2 tablespoons cocoa
- 2 tablespoons butter, melted
- 1 teaspoon vanilla
- 1/2 cup nonfat milk

Cocoa Mix:
- 1/2 cup sugar
- 1/4 cup cocoa
- 1/2 cup brown sugar
- 1 cup cold water

Sift together flour, salt, sugar, baking powder and cocoa. Combine melted butter, vanilla and milk with dry ingredients; pour into buttered 8" x 8" baking dish. In another bowl, combine ingredients for Cocoa Mix. Pour cocoa mix over batter in baking dish and shake to cover. Pour cold water over top (it looks weird!). Bake at 350 degrees for 30 minutes. Invert into sherbet glass. Serve warm or cold.

"Chocoholics will like this - very rich but only 2 tablespoons of butter. If you're not worried about fat - add 1/2 cup chopped nuts or top with vanilla ice cream or whipping cream."
Amber Bradley   Granite Hills High School, El Cajon, CA

Cranberry Apple Snack Cut-Outs

Makes 48   *20 calories, 0 fat grams*

nonstick cooking spray
1 (12 ounce) can frozen cranberry juice concentrate, thawed
1 1/2 cups apple juice
3 envelopes unflavored gelatin

Lightly spray a 13" x 9" pan with nonstick cooking spray. In medium saucepan, combine juices; sprinkle with gelatin. Allow to soften 1 to 2 minutes. Cook over medium heat until gelatin dissolves, stirring constantly. Pour into pan and refrigerate until firm (up to 2 hours). Cut into desired shapes with your favorite cookie cutters.

"My students enjoy combining their creativity with this good healthy recipe. Valentine's Day is especially fun to cut out heart shapes, frost with pink tinted Cool Whip and decorate to share in class."
Shirley Blough   Hillside Junior High School, Simi Valley, CA

Double Boiler Rice Pudding

Serves 8   *204 calories, 3 fat grams*

1/2 cup uncooked rice
3 cups boiling water
1/2 teaspoon salt
1 (15 ounce) can low or nonfat sweetened condensed milk
1/4 cup margarine
1/4 cup raisins
1 teaspoon vanilla

Measure rice, boiling water and salt into top of double boiler. Cook over rapidly boiling water until rice is tender, about 40 minutes. Stir in sweetened condensed milk, margarine and raisins. Cook, stirring frequently, until slightly thickened, about 20 minutes. Remove from heat and stir in vanilla. Serve warm or cold.

"This is the best rice pudding and always a hit whenever it is served."
Vicki Pearl   Giano Middle School, La Puente, CA

Easy Baked Apples

Serves 8   *70 calories, 0 fat grams*

4 Rome Beauty apples
1 can diet black cherry soda
cinnamon

Cut apples in half and remove core. Place, cut side up, in 9" x 13" pan. Pour soda over and around apples and sprinkle with cinnamon. Cover with foil and bake at 350 degrees for 45 to 50 minutes or until apples are tender. Serve warm or chilled.

"This is another of my all-time favorite Weight Watcher's recipes. You won't believe how good these are!"
Penny Niadna   **Golden West High School, Visalia, CA**

Easy Fruit Tarts

Serves 12   *55 calories, 0 fat grams*

12 wonton skins
nonstick cooking spray
2 tablespoons apple jelly or apricot fruit spread
1 cup nonfat or lowfat yogurt, any flavor
1 1/2 cups assorted fruit, sliced or cut up, such as Dole bananas, strawberries,
   raspberries, nectarines, red or green seedless grapes

Press wonton skin into each of 12 muffin cups that have been sprayed with nonstick cooking spray. Allow corners of wontons to extend over edges of muffin cups. Bake at 375 degrees for 6 to 8 minutes or until lightly browned. Carefully remove wonton cups to wire rack; cool. Cook and stir jelly in small saucepan over low heat until jelly melts. Brush bottoms of cooled wonton cups with melted jelly. Place 2 fruit slices in each cup; spoon rounded tablespoon of yogurt over fruit. Garnish with additional fruit slices, if desired. Serve immediately.
Dole Food Company

Fat Free Cherry Cheesecake

Serves 10   *200 calories, 2.5 fat grams*

3 (8 ounce) packages cream cheese, fat free
3/4 cup sugar
1 teaspoon vanilla
3 eggs
nonstick cooking spray
1/3 cup graham cracker crumbs
1 (20 ounce) can reduced calorie cherry pie filling

With electric mixer, blend together cream cheese, sugar and vanilla at medium speed. Add eggs. Mix just until blended - do not overbeat. Spray 9" pie plate with nonstick cooking spray. Sprinkle bottom of pan with crumbs. Pour cream cheese mixture into prepared pie plate. Bake at 325 degrees for 45 minutes or until center is almost set. Cool. Refrigerate 3 hours or overnight. Top with pie filling.
Lura Staffanson   **Centennial High School, Corona, CA**

Fat Free Rice Krispy Treats

Serves 16   *100 calories, 0 fat grams*

nonstick cooking spray
1 (10 ounce) package marshmallows
3 tablespoons butter flavor sprinkles
3/4 teaspoon water
3/4 teaspoon vanilla
6 cups crisp rice cereal

Spray 13" x 9" x 2" pan and large saucepan with nonstick cooking spray. Melt marshmallows over low heat, stirring until smooth. Add butter sprinkles, water and vanilla; mix well. Add cereal and stir quickly until well coated. Press into pan; cool. Cut into 16 squares.

"This is a favorite with the teenagers."
Bonnie Shrock   **Kearny High School, San Diego, CA**

Fresh Berry Cheese Cake

Serves 12   *100 calories, 3 fat grams*

nonstick cooking spray
1/4 cup cornstarch
1/3 cup sugar
1 tablespoon flour
1 1/2 cups lowfat or part skim ricotta cheese
1 1/2 cups lowfat cottage cheese
1/2 cup plain nonfat yogurt
1 teaspoon vanilla
1 1/2 teaspoons lemon peel, grated
2 large eggs, separated
1 large egg white
fresh berries

Preheat oven to 350 degrees. Spray 9" springform pan with cooking spray. Wrap outside of pan with heavy-duty foil. Combine cornstarch, sugar and flour in a small bowl. In a food processor, combine cheese, yogurt, vanilla, lemon peel and egg yolks; pulse until smooth. Add flour mixture and pulse until smooth. Pour into large bowl. Beat egg whites to soft peaks - fold in batter and pour into prepared pan. Place pan in a larger baking pan. Place pans on oven rack. Pour boiling water into large pan to reach 1" up side of pan. Bake 30 minutes, until just firm in center. Cool on wire rack. Refrigerate until chilled about 3 hours. Serve with berries.

Marjorie Brown   **Cabrillo High School, Lompoc, CA**

Ice Milk Fruit Sundae
9 fat grams, see page 131

Easy Fruit Tarts
0 fat grams, see page 127

Light & Easy Chocolate Angel Cake
    0 fat grams
Light & Easy Chocolate Mousse
    1.5 fat grams
see pages 132–133

Fruit Pizza

Serves 12   *157 calories, 5 fat grams*

1 (20 ounce) package refrigerated chocolate chip cookie dough, reduced fat
3 cups cool whip topping, light, thawed
1 banana, sliced
1 kiwi, sliced
8 medium strawberries, sliced
2 slices pineapple, sliced
1/2 cup seedless grapes, halved

Preheat oven to 350 degrees. Press dough evenly into 12" pizza pan. Bake 15 to 20 minutes or until golden brown. Cool in pan on wire rack. Slide cooled cookie crust on serving plate. Spread whipped topping on cookie crust. Garnish with fruit. Serve immediately or refrigerate until ready to use.

"This is a favorite for dessert. Any flavor cookie dough may be used. When fresh fruit is out of season, use canned. Be sure it is drained."
Gerry Henderson   **Temple City High School, Temple City,**

Ginger Lime Cheesecake

Serves 12   *117 calories, 5 fat grams*

nonstick cooking spray
1 tablespoon unsalted butter
4 zwieback toasts, finely crumbled
1/2 cup brown sugar, firmly packed
1 1/2 teaspoons lime rind, grated
1 teaspoon ginger, ground
3 tablespoons lime juice
2 envelopes unflavored gelatin
2 cups part skim ricotta cheese
1 cup lowfat yogurt, plain
1/2 cup nonfat milk
1 large egg yolk

Coat an 8"springform pan with nonstick cooking spray and set aside. Melt butter and mix in zwieback toasts crumbs, 1 teaspoon brown sugar, 1/2 teaspoon lime rind and 1/4 teaspoon ginger. Press mixture evenly over bottom of pan and refrigerate while you prepare filling. Place lime juice in a heatproof glass measuring cup; sprinkle gelatin on top and let stand at room temperature until softened, about 5 minutes. In shallow saucepan, bring about 1 cup water to a simmer over moderately high heat . Place measuring cup with gelatin in gently bubbling water, adjust heat to low and stir until gelatin dissolves completely, about 4 minutes. Remove from heat and set aside. In a food processor or blender, combine ricotta cheese, yogurt, remaining 1/2 cup brown sugar and milk and blend until smooth, about 1 minute. Add egg yolk, remaining 1 teaspoon lime rind and remaining 3/4 teaspoon ginger; blend 1 minute more. Add cooled gelatin mixture and blend 15 seconds longer. Gently pour cheese mixture over crust in pan and refrigerate at least 5 hours or until set.

"We love the 10 minute preparation time for this easy but elegant dessert."
Sue Walters   **Morse High School, San Diego, CA**

Gingerbread Drop Cookies

Makes 4 dozen   *50 calories, 1 fat gram*

nonstick cooking spray
$1/3$ cup butter, softened
$2/3$ cup brown sugar, packed
1 teaspoon baking soda
1 $1/2$ teaspoons cinnamon, divided
1 teaspoon ground ginger
1 egg
$1/4$ cup molasses
1 $1/2$ cups all-purpose flour
$1/2$ cup whole wheat flour
$1/4$ cup sugar

Spray cookie sheet with nonstick cooking spray and set aside. In large mixing bowl, beat butter with an electric mixer on medium to high speed for 30 seconds. Add brown sugar, baking soda, 1/2 teaspoon cinnamon and ginger. Beat until creamy. Beat in egg and molasses. Beat in as much of the two flours as possible while mixer is running. Stir in any remaining flour. Cover and chill in refrigerator for one hour. Shape dough into 1" balls. Combine the granulated sugar and remaining 1 teaspoon cinnamon. Roll balls in cinnamon-sugar mixture. Place balls 2" apart on prepared cookie sheet. Bake at 350 degrees for 10 to 11 minutes or until set and the tops are cracked. Remove from cookie sheet and cool on wire rack.

Pam Ford   **Temecula Valley High School, Temecula, CA**

Healthy Double Chocolate Chip Cookies

Makes 24   *40 calories, 2 fat grams*

$1/2$ cup brown sugar
$1/4$ cup butter
$1/2$ teaspoon vanilla
1 egg white
1 cup flour
3 tablespoons unsweetened cocoa
$1/2$ teaspoon baking soda
$1/8$ teaspoon salt
$1/2$ cup semi-sweet chocolate chips

Heat oven to 375 degrees. In a large bowl, beat brown sugar and butter until light and fluffy. Add vanilla and egg white. Blend well. Add flour, cocoa, baking soda and salt. Mix well. Stir in chocolate chips. Drop by teaspoonfuls 2" apart onto ungreased cookie sheets. Bake for 8 to 9 minutes or until set. Do not overbake! Cool 1 minute. Remove from cookie sheet.

Patti Bartholomew   Casa Roble High School, Orangevale, CA

Ice Milk Fruit Sundae

Serves 1   *512 calories, 9 fat grams*

1 1/2 cups ice milk
1/4 cup strawberry sauce (recipe below)
fresh strawberries, sliced
fresh kiwi fruit, sliced
fresh raspberries
fresh blueberries
fresh peach slices
mint sprigs, for garnish
Strawberry Sauce:
3 cups fresh strawberries, hulled
1/3 cup sugar
1 tablespoon lemon juice
1 tablespoon cornstarch
2 to 3 drops red food coloring

Prepare strawberry sauce by crushing strawberries, straining through a ricer, then through a fine sieve, reserving juice. Add sugar, lemon juice, cornstarch and food coloring to berries and juice and cook, stirring, over low heat, until sauce becomes thick and transparent. Set aside to cool. Scoop ice cream into sundae glass. Top with strawberry sauce and fresh fruit. Serve!

Wisconsin Milk Marketing Board

Lemon Bisque

Serves 8   *217 calories, 8 fat grams*

1 can evaporated milk
1 package lemon gelatin
3/4 cup boiling water
1/2 cup sugar
14 to 15 graham crackers
1/4 cup butter or margarine
1/3 cup lemon juice

Chill can of evaporated milk until ice crystals form (about 1 hour in freezer). Chill mixing bowl and beaters. Meanwhile, dissolve gelatin in boiling water, add sugar and stir well. Chill, stirring occasionally until gelatin becomes syrupy. Do not let it jell completely. Place graham crackers in plastic bag and roll until finely crushed. Melt margarine and mix with cracker crumbs. Put 1/2 to 3/4 cracker crumb mixture into bottom of a rectangular

Light **&** ***Delicious***

cake pan. Remove canned milk from freezer and beat in chilled mixing bowl until very fluffy and stiff. Add lemon juice and set aside. Whip gelatin mixture and fold into whipped milk. Pour into pan and spread evenly. Top with remaining crumbs. Chill before serving.

"The only fat is in the crust. Light and delicious! Lime gelatin can be used."
Judy Hammann   Mesa Junior High School, Mesa, AZ

Lemon Rice Pudding

Serves 8   *141 calories, 1 fat gram*

- 1 ¹/₂ cups water
- ¹/₂ cup long grain rice, uncooked
- ¹/₃ cup raisins
- ¹/₄ teaspoon ground nutmeg
- 1 (1 ounce) package sugar free vanilla pudding mix
- 2 cups nonfat milk
- 2 teaspoons lemon peel, grated

In a saucepan, bring water, rice, raisins and nutmeg to a boil. Reduce heat; cover and simmer for 15 to 20 minutes until all liquid is absorbed; cool. Prepare pudding mix according to directions on the box. Stir in rice mixture and lemon peel. Serve immediately or refrigerate.
Pat Smith   Kern Valley High School, Lake Isabella, CA

Light & Easy Chocolate Cheese Filled Angel Cake

Serves 18   *120 calories, 0 fat grams*

- ¹/₂ cup yogurt cheese*
- 1 (10 ") white angel food cake
- ¹/₃ cup sugar
- 3 tablespoons Hershey's European-Style Cocoa or Hershey's Cocoa
- 2 tablespoons hot water
- 1 ¹/₂ teaspoons vanilla, divided
- 1 (1.3 ounce) envelope dry whipped topping mix
- ¹/₂ cup cold nonfat milk

Prepare yogurt cheese: use 1 (8 ounce) container plain nonfat yogurt, no gelatin added. Line non-rusting colander or sieve with large coffee filter; place over deep bowl. Spoon yogurt into prepared colander; cover with plastic wrap. Refrigerate until liquid no longer drains from yogurt, about 12 hours. Remove yogurt from colander; discard liquid. Refrigerate. Cut angel food cake into 3 horizontal layers. In small bowl, stir together sugar, cocoa and hot water until smooth; stir in 1 teaspoon vanilla. Stir in yogurt cheese until well blended. Prepare whipped topping mix as directed on package, using 1/2 cup milk and remaining 1/2 teaspoon vanilla; fold into cocoa mixture. Spread cocoa mixture between layers and on top and sides of cake. Cover; refrigerate.
Hershey Foods Corporation

132

Light & Easy Fruited Chocolate Mousse

Serves 8   *110 calories, 1.5 fat grams*

1 (3 ounce) package strawberry flavored gelatin
³/₄ cup boiling water
¹/₄ cup Hershey's European Style Cocoa or Hershey's Cocoa
1 cup ice cubes
1 (10 ounce) package frozen strawberries in syrup, thawed and well drained
¹/₂ cup frozen light non-dairy whipped topping, thawed

In blender container, place gelatin; carefully pour in boiling water. Cover; blend on low speed until gelatin in completely dissolved. Add cocoa; continue blending until smooth. Immediately add ice cubes, blending until melted. Add strawberries and light whipped topping; continue blending, just until combined and smooth. Immediately pour into dessert dishes; refrigerate until set, about 4 hours.
Hershey's Foods Corporation

Lisa Snasdell's Low Fat Cheese Cake

Serves 12   *245 calories, 12 fat grams*

2 (8 ounce) packages fat free cream cheese, softened
1 egg white
¹/₂ cup liquid egg substitute
³/₄ cup sugar
1 teaspoon vanilla
Keebler lowfat graham cracker crust
blueberry pie filling

Beat together cream cheese, egg white, egg substitute, sugar and vanilla until well blended. Pour into prepared pie crust and bake at 350 degrees for 1 hour, or until knife inserted in center comes out clean. When cooled, top with pie filling and chill at least one hour.

"Mrs. Snasdell is a parent volunteer in my class. She developed this recipe when she started watching her fat grams. I tried a piece, and it is great!"
Phyllis Greer   Vista Verde Middle School, Moreno Valley, CA

Lowfat Carrot Cake

Serves 16   *218 calories, 5 fat grams*

2 1/2 cups flour
2 tablespoons baking soda
2 teaspoons cinnamon
1 teaspoon ginger
1/2 teaspoon allspice
1/2 teaspoon salt
1 cup brown sugar
1/4 cup vegetable oil
2 eggs or equivalent egg substitute
1/2 cup nonfat yogurt, plain
3 carrots, grated
1/2 cup raisins
1 small can crushed pineapple, drained

Combine dry ingredients in a bowl. In another large bowl, combine brown sugar, oil, eggs and yogurt. Fold in carrots, raisins and pineapple, stir in flour. Pour into a greased 13" x 9" pan. Bake at 350 degrees for 35 - 40 minutes. NOTE: Frost with a cream cheese frosting made with lowfat or nonfat cream cheese.

"This is the best carrot cake - it does not taste lowfat!"
Cynthia Allen   **Sinaloa Junior High School, Simi Valley, CA**

Lowfat Pumpkin Pie

Serves 8   *222 calories, 7 fat grams*

3/4 cup gingersnaps, crushed
1/2 cup crushed graham crackers, crushed
1 tablespoon sugar
1 tablespoon flour
3 tablespoons margarine, melted
1 (16 ounce) can pumpkin
1/2 cup brown sugar
2 teaspoons pumpkin pie spice
3/4 cup liquid egg substitute
1 cup evaporated skim milk

Mix first 5 ingredients together and press into 9" pie pan; chill 1 hour. In mixing bowl, combine the next 3 ingredients. Beat in egg substitute; gradually add milk. Pour into pie shell. Bake at 375 degrees for 45 minutes or until center is set when gently shaken.

"Yummy and lots lower in fat than regular pumpkin pie. Serve with light whipped topping, if desired."
Jane Souza   **North Monterey County High School, Castroville, CA**

Miss Piggy's Secret Cookies

Makes 4 dozen   *90 calories, 2 fat grams*

nonstick cooking spray
1/2 cup light corn oil spread
3/4 cup dark brown sugar, firmly packed
1/2 cup sugar
2 large egg whites
1 large whole egg
2 teaspoons vanilla
2 cups all-purpose flour
1 teaspoon baking soda
1/2 teaspoon salt
1 cup uncooked quick oats
1 cup lowfat semi-sweet chocolate pieces
1/2 cup seedless raisins

Preheat oven to 375 degrees. Spray 2 large cookie sheets with the nonstick spray. In large bowl, mix corn oil spread and both sugars at low speed until combined. Increase mixer speed to high and beat until light and fluffy. Add egg whites, egg and vanilla; beat until smooth. Add the dry ingredients and blend. Fold in chips and raisins and gently mix until well blended. Drop by level tablespoons about 2" apart on baking pan. Bake 10 - 12 minutes; remove to wire racks to cool. Store tightly covered.

"With these delicious cookies, you won't become a Miss Piggy look-alike."
Sally Reimers   Valley View Junior High School, Simi Valley, CA

Mom's Best Brownies

Makes 12   *112 calories, 4 fat grams*

nonstick cooking spray
1/2 cup cake flour, sifted
1/2 cup unsweetened cocoa powder
1/4 teaspoon salt
2 egg whites
1 large egg
3/4 cup granulated sugar
6 tablespoons unsweetened applesauce
1 tablespoon vegetable oil
1 1/2 teaspoons vanilla
1 tablespoon walnuts, chopped (optional)

Preheat oven to 350 degrees. Spray an 8" square baking pan with nonstick spray and set aside. In a medium bowl, combine flour, cocoa and salt. Mix well. In a large bowl, whisk together egg whites, egg, sugar, applesauce, oil and vanilla. Stir in flour mixture until just blended; do not over mix. Pour batter into prepared pan; sprinkle with walnuts. Bake until just set and toothpick inserted in center comes out clean, about 25 minutes. Place pan on wire rack and cool for at least 15 minutes.

"Indulge yourself - lower cholesterol, reduced sugar and almost fat free!"
Phyllis Miller   **Buena High School, Ventura, CA**

No-Fat Chocolate Cake

Serves 8   *220 calories, .8 fat grams*

1 cup cake flour, sifted
$1/3$ cup unsweetened cocoa
1 teaspoon baking soda
1 teaspoon baking powder
6 large egg whites
1 $1/2$ cups brown sugar, firmly packed
1 cup unflavored nonfat yogurt
1 teaspoon vanilla
powdered sugar

Mix flour, cocoa, baking soda, and baking powder together; set aside. In a large bowl, beat egg whites, brown sugar, yogurt and vanilla until well blended. Stir in flour mixture and beat until evenly moistened. Pour batter into a nonstick 8" square pan (or coat an unfinished pan lightly with cooking oil spray and dust with flour). Bake at 350 degrees for 30 to 40 minutes, or until cake springs back when lightly pressed in center. Let cake cool for 15 minutes, then invert it onto a serving plate. Sift powdered sugar over cake (if desired, use a doily as stencil for pattern). Serve warm or cool. If made ahead, wrap airtight and store in a cool place up to 2 days. Cut into squares.

Sheryal Walther   **Lakewood High School, Lakewood, CA**

Nonfat Lemon Cheesecake

Serves 16   *175 calories, 0 fat grams*

nonstick cooking spray
12 raspberry fat free Newtons
6 egg whites, stiffly beaten
32 ounces fat free cream cheese, softened
1 cup sugar
4 tablespoons flour
1 cup nonfat sour cream
2 tablespoons lemon juice
1 teaspoon lemon peel, grated

Spray sides and bottom of 9" springform pan with nonstick cooking spray. Press Newtons flat in bottom of pan, covering surface. Beat egg whites until stiff; set aside. In mixer, whip together cream cheese, sugar, flour, sour cream, lemon juice and lemon peel until fluffy. Fold egg whites into mixture. Pour into springform pan. Bake at 450 degrees for first 10 minutes, reduce heat to 250 degrees and continue to cook for 1 hour.

136   **Betty Wells**   **Oroville High School, Oroville, CA**

Orange Banana Pop

Serves 6   *77 calories, 0 fat grams*

3 medium bananas, mashed
1 cup unsweetened orange juice
1/4 cup water
1 teaspoon lime juice
1/4 teaspoon powdered sweetener

Beat all ingredients at low speed with an electric mixer. Pour into six 5 ounce paper cups. Freeze until a wooden stick inserted into center of cup remains standing. Freeze until firm. To serve, let pop stand at room temperature for 5 minutes. Peel away the cup before eating.

"This is a fun recipe for youngsters to help make."
Alice Demele   **Colton High School, Colton, CA**

Peach Blintzes

Serves 6   *191 calories, 0 fat grams*

Peach Filling:
1 1/2 cups nonfat yogurt
2 tablespoons peach nectar
1/4 teaspoon cinnamon
1 cup peaches, sliced
Blintzes:
4 egg whites
2 cups nonfat milk
1 tablespoon peach nectar
1 1/2 cups whole wheat flour
1/2 teaspoon baking powder
nonstick cooking spray

To make filling: Place yogurt in a strainer lined with a paper coffee filter. Suspend over a bowl, cover with plastic wrap. Refrigerate and allow to drain overnight. Put the resulting yogurt cheese into a medium bowl. Stir in nectar and cinnamon. Fold in peaches; set aside. To make blintzes: In a medium bowl, whisk egg whites until frothy. Whisk in milk and nectar. Add flour and baking powder; mix well. Coat a small nonstick skillet with cooking spray. Place over medium heat for a few minutes. Add about 1/4 cup batter to pan and tilt the pan in all directions to spread the batter thinly over bottom. Cook for about 1 minute, or until browned on the underside. Carefully flip the blintz and brown the other side for about 30 seconds. Turn blintz onto wire rack. Repeat procedure until you've used all the batter - you'll have about 12 blintzes. To serve: Spoon about 1/8 cup of the peach filling down the center of each blintz. Fold in the sides carefully. Transfer blintzes, seam side down, to individual plates. With filling left over, dab the top of each blintz.

Ruth Mills   **Los Alisos Intermediate School, Mission Viejo, CA**

Peaches & Cream

Serves 6   *342 calories, 11 fat grams*

1 small package instant vanilla pudding
3/4 cup self-rising flour
1/2 cup nonfat milk
1 egg
3 tablespoons margarine, melted
1 (30 ounce) can peaches, in light syrup, drained (reserve 3 tablespoons syrup)
1 (8 ounce) fat free cream cheese
1/2 cup sugar (or less)
cinnamon sugar for garnish

In mixer bowl, combine vanilla pudding mix, flour, milk, egg and margarine. Beat for 2 minutes, then spread into 11" x 8" pan. Drain peaches, reserving 3 tablespoon juice. Arrange peach slices over pudding mixture. Beat cream cheese, sugar and reserved juice together and spread on top of mixture. Sprinkle with cinnamon sugar and bake at 350 degrees for 40 minutes. Serve hot or cold.

Carol Kagy   Norwalk High School, Norwalk, CA

Pear-Berry Sorbet

Serves 6   *56 calories, 0 fat grams*

2 fresh Bartlett pears
1 1/2 tablespoons lemon juice
2 cups fresh strawberries or 8 ounces unsweetened frozen strawberries
1/2 cup nonfat milk
3 teaspoons sugar

Pare, core and coarsely chop pears; toss with lemon juice. Spread pears on baking sheet. Freeze, uncovered, until frozen solid. If using fresh strawberries, freeze along with pears. Place frozen fruit in food processor or blender. Add milk and sugar; process until smooth. Serve immediately.

"A great recipe for cholesterol watchers!"
Kathy Warren   McClatchy High School, Sacramento, CA

Pineapple Cream Cake

Serves 16   *206 calories, 4 fat grams*

1 (18.5 ounce) package light yellow cake mix
3 egg whites
1 1/3 cups water
nonstick cooking spray
2 cups nonfat milk
1 (3.4 ounce) instant banana pudding and pie filling
1 (15 ounce) can unsweetened crushed pineapple, well drained
2 cups whipped topping

Mix the first 3 ingredients in a large bowl; beat with an electric mixer at low speed, 30 seconds, then increase to medium speed and beat 2 minutes. Pour mixture into a 13" x 9" x 2" baking pan that has been coated with nonstick cooking spray. Bake at 350 degrees for 35 minutes. Mix milk and pudding mix at low speed 2 minutes, or until thickened. Cover and refrigerate 5 minutes. Stir in pineapple. Poke holes in top of cake with a fork. Spread pudding over cake and then spread the whipped topping over the pudding. Store in refrigerator.

"Sliced almonds or toasted coconut may be sprinkled on top, if desired, but they will add calories and fat. This is a quick and easy dessert, low in fat, without almonds and coconut."
Judith Huffman   **Mariposa High School, Mariposa, CA**

Pumpkin Pie Cake

Serves 8   *383 calories, 11 fat grams*

    nonstick cooking spray
    1 (29 ounce) can pumpkin puree
    1 cup liquid egg substitute
    1 1/4 cups sugar
    1 (12 ounce) can evaporated skim milk
    2 teaspoons cinnamon
    1 package yellow cake mix
    1/4 cup walnuts, chopped
    1/2 cup reduced calorie margarine, melted
    3/4 cup nonfat milk

Heat oven to 350 degrees. Lightly spray 9" x 13" pan with nonstick cooking spray. Using mixer, beat together pumpkin puree, egg substitute, sugar, evaporated milk and cinnamon. In a separate bowl stir cake mix, nuts, margarine and nonfat milk to make a thick batter. Pour pumpkin mixture into pan. Spoon batter over pumpkin. Bake 1 hour, or until cake is firm. Cool completely before serving.

"This tastes like pumpkin pie - and tastes even better after it sets for a day!"
Libby Newman   **West Valley High School, Hemet, CA**

Pumpkin Snack Cake

Serves 12   *170 calories, 3 fat grams*

nonstick cooking spray
1 cup brown sugar, firmly packed
4 tablespoons light corn-oil spread
1 cup canned pumpkin
$1/2$ cup egg substitute
$1/2$ cup lowfat milk
1 tablespoon vanilla
2 cups cake flour
2 teaspoons baking soda
1 $1/2$ teaspoons cinnamon
1 $1/2$ teaspoons ground ginger
$1/2$ teaspoon allspice
1 teaspoon baking powder
$1/2$ teaspoon salt

Preheat oven to 350 degrees. Generously coat a 13" x 9" glass baking dish with nonstick cooking spray. In a large bowl with mixer on high, beat brown sugar and corn oil spread until well mixed, about 2 minutes. Reduce speed to medium; beat in pumpkin, egg substitute, milk and vanilla. Turn mixer on low, add remaining dry ingredients. Beat until well blended. Pour into baking dish and spread evenly. Bake 25 to 30 minutes or until a toothpick inserted in center comes out clean. Cool completely. Sprinkle with confectioner's sugar.

"Moist and tasty."
Carol Ballard   Eureka High School, Eureka, CA

Raspberry Crepe Delight

Serves 6   *328 calories, 11 fat grams*

2 eggs
1 cup nonfat milk
3 tablespoons margarine, melted
$1/4$ teaspoon salt
$1/2$ cup flour
1 teaspoon vanilla
nonstick cooking spray
$1/2$ cup Hershey's chocolate syrup
3 cups Dreyer's No Sugar/No Fat Vanilla ice cream
raspberries, unsweetened
6 tablespoons light whipped topping

Blend first 6 ingredients in a blender until smooth. Heat a 6" skillet on medium heat. Spray nonstick cooking spray over surface for each crepe. Cook each crepe approximately 1 minute on each side until golden brown.

Layer each crepe between paper towels and refrigerate until ready to use. Set on counter 1/2 hour before using to bring to room temperature. To serve, zig zag chocolate syrup across each serving plate. Fill each crepe with 2 (small) scoops ice cream and fold over sides. Place in middle of chocolate zig zags. Top with raspberries and a small dollop of whipping cream.

"Pretty on the plate and light and delightful to eat!"
Gail McAuley   Lincoln High School, Stockton, CA

Raspberry Peach Melba

Serves 4   *92 calories, 0 fat grams*

　4 fresh peaches, peeled, pitted and halved
　lemon juice
　1/2 cup low-sugar raspberry jam
　1 cup prepared low-calorie whipped topping

Arrange peaches in a 2" x 8" baking dish. Brush with lemon juice to prevent discoloration. Cover with plastic wrap and microwave at high for 2 - 6 minutes, or until soft, turning dish a quarter halfway through cooking; cool. Microwave jam in a 1 cup measure at HIGH 30 - 60 seconds, or until thinned, stirring once. Place 2 peach halves in each of 4 serving dishes. Top each with 1/4 cup whipped topping, then 2 tablespoons heated jam. Serve immediately. Variation: substitute 1 (16 ounce) can peaches for fresh. During first cooking span - microwave only until warm, about 1 minute.

"You can use "Simply Fruit" raspberry topping to cut down on sugar and calories."
Rita Blohm   Nogales High School, La Puente, CA

Razzleberry Trifle

Serves 10   *191 calories, 1 fat gram*

　2 1/2 cups fresh strawberries, sliced
　1 cup fresh or frozen raspberries, thawed
　2 tablespoons sugar
　1 (6 serving) package instant vanilla pudding mix
　3 cups nonfat milk
　10 slices (1/2" thick) fat free loaf cake
　1/4 cup low sugar raspberry jam
　Topping:
　3/4 cup light Cool Whip topping
　3/4 cup nonfat vanilla yogurt

Combine strawberries, raspberries and sugar in a medium sized bowl and stir to mix well; set aside for 20 minutes to develop juice. Prepare pudding with skim milk according to package directions; set aside. Spread one side of each cake slice with a thin layer of jam. Arrange half the slices over bottom of a 3 quart trifle bowl. Top with half of fruit mixture and then with half of pudding; repeat layers. To make topping, place cool whip in a small bowl and fold in the yogurt. Swirl this mixture over the top of the trifle. Cover and chill for at least 2 hours.

"This recipe came from my favorite sister-in-law, Berta Schumacher, who has become famous for her delicious lowfat, low calorie recipes."
Kay Linberger   Tokay High School, Lodi, CA

Reduced Fat Brownies

Makes 36   *118 calories, 5 fat grams*

nonstick cooking spray
3/4 cup cocoa
1/2 teaspoon baking soda
2/3 cup lowfat margarine, melted
1/2 cup boiling water
2 cups sugar
3 egg whites
1 teaspoon vanilla
1 1/3 cups flour, sifted
1/4 teaspoon salt
1 cup Hershey's reduced fat semi-sweet baking chips

Preheat oven to 350 degrees. Spray 13" x 9" baking pan with nonstick cooking spray. In large bowl, stir together cocoa and baking soda; stir in 1/3 cup melted margarine. Add boiling water; stir until mixture thickens. Stir in sugar, egg whites, vanilla and remaining 1/3 cup melted margarine. Stir until smooth. Add flour and salt and blend completely. Stir in baking chips; pour into prepared pan. Bake 30 to 35 minutes or until brownies begin to pull away from sides of pan. Cool completely in pan on wire rack. Cut into squares. Store in airtight container.
Carol Goddard   Alhambra High School, Alhambra, CA

Sherbet Lite

Serves 16   *144 calories, 2 fat grams*

1/2 gallon pineapple sherbet
juice of 1 orange
juice of 1/2 lemon
1 large container Cool Whip Lite

Soften sherbet and combine with remaining ingredients. Spoon into individual dessert dishes or large container and refreeze.

"Very light and mild flavored. Not as sweet as sherbet or as heavy as ice cream. A wonderful dessert after a heavy or spicy meal."
Sandra Dennis   Mt. Carmel High School, San Diego, CA

Strawberry Angel Food Cake

Serves 12   *263 calories, 6 fat grams*

1 (.6 ounce) package sugar free strawberry jello
2 ½ cups boiling water
2 (10 ounce) packages frozen strawberries, sliced
¼ cup sugar
⅛ teaspoon salt
1 large angel food cake, torn into bite-sized pieces
1 (8 ounce) carton "light" Cool Whip

Dissolve jello in boiling water. Stir in strawberries, sugar and salt. Cool mixture until thickened. Fold in Cool Whip. Place torn pieces of cake in 9" x 13" pan. Pour strawberry jello mixture over the cake. Refrigerate until firm.

"A refreshing light dessert, especially good in the summertime. Recipe was given to me by my good friend, Cherie Manning. Original recipe called for a 6 ounce package of regular jello and 1 pint of whipping cream."
Susan Lefler   Ramona Junior High School, Chino, CA

Strawberry Daiquiri Pie

Serves 12   *263 calories, 2 fat grams*

1 pint mango sorbet
2 pints vanilla frozen yogurt
1 large graham cracker crust
1 (10 ounce) frozen nonalcoholic strawberry daiquiri mixer
1 pint strawberries

Allow sorbet and frozen yogurt to soften at room temperature 15 or 20 minutes. Spread mango sorbet over bottom of graham cracker crust. Put vanilla frozen yogurt in bowl. Spoon in all but 1/4 cup of frozen daiquiri mixer. With rubber spatula, swirl it though the frozen yogurt for a marble effect. Spread over mango sorbet. Cover and freeze until ready to serve, at least 1 hour or up to 4 days. Put remaining 1/4 cup daiquiri mixer in bowl. Mash 1/2 cup strawberries into daiquiri mixer. Slice remaining berries in half and add. Cover and refrigerate up to 8 hours. Shortly before serving, top pie with some of the strawberry mixture. Serve remaining berry mixture to spoon over servings.

"A terrific summer cooler dessert!"
Margaret McLeod   Nogales High School, La Puente, CA

Strawberry Pineapple Shortcake

Serves 8   *113 calories, 0 fat grams*

1 (3 ounce) package sugar free strawberry gelatin
3/4 cup boiling water
1 (8 ounce) package frozen unsweetened strawberries, sliced
1 (15 1/4 ounce) can crushed pineapple, packed in juice, not drained
1 tablespoon lemon juice
8 (1 ounce) slices angel food cake

Dissolve gelatin in boiling water, stirring until all lumps are gone. (If strawberries are whole, slice into small pieces.) Add strawberries to gelatin and stir until thawed. Stir in undrained pineapple and lemon juice; chill. Just before serving, stir gelatin mixture and top cake slices with sauce.

Robin Ali-Christie   Nevada Union High School, Grass Valley, CA

Sugarless Apple Pie

Serves 8   *239 calories, 12 fat grams*

9" pie crust for double crust pie
1 (6 ounce) can apple juice, frozen
3 cups apples, sliced
3/4 teaspoon cinnamon
1 tablespoon cornstarch
2 tablespoons water
1 tablespoon butter
1 tablespoon nonfat milk

Preheat oven to 350 degrees. Prepare pie crust. Place bottom crust in pie pan; set aside. Heat apple juice and apples in covered saucepan; simmer until tender. Add cinnamon. Stir in cornstarch which has been moistened with a little cold water. Fill pie shell, dot with butter and cover with remaining crust. Make holes in top crust. Brush with milk and bake for 30 minutes.

Kathy Croxall   Fontana High School, Fontana, CA

Susie's Oatmeal-Walnut Cookies

Makes 24 cookies   *150 calories, 3 fat grams*

2 cups oatmeal
1 1/2 cups flour
1 cup brown sugar, firmly packed
1 cup walnuts, chopped
1 cup light Karo syrup
1/2 cup applesauce
1 teaspoon salt
1 teaspoon baking soda
1 teaspoon vanilla

Combine dry ingredients in a large bowl. In another bowl, stir together remaining ingredients, then pour into dry ingredients and blend thoroughly. Drop dough onto greased cookie sheets about 2" apart. Bake at 375 degrees for 10 - 15 minutes.

"In a quest for fitness and health, I created this recipe in order to indulge in oatmeal cookies with very low fat and plenty of nutritional value. I love 'em!"
Sue Zallar   Capistrano Valley High School, Mission Viejo, CA

Yogurt Fruit Pie

Serves 6   *218 calories, 9 fat grams*

1 package graham crackers
2 tablespoons margarine, melted
1 package gelatin
1/2 cup orange juice
8 ounces nonfat cream cheese
8 ounces nonfat plain yogurt
1/2 cup sugar
assorted fresh fruits for garnish, sliced
1 tablespoon apple jelly, melted

Prepare graham cracker crust by combining graham cracker crumbs with melted margarine and pressing into 9" pie pan; set aside. Sprinkle gelatin over orange juice and let stand 1 minute, then microwave until melted. Beat cream cheese, yogurt and sugar until smooth. Beat in gelatin mixture until light and bubbly. Arrange fresh fruit on top. Place apple jelly in small microwave dish and cook on HIGH about 25 - 30 seconds, or until melted. Brush over fruit arranged on top of pie. Refrigerate until ready to serve.
Donna Swennes   El Capitan High School, Lakeside, CA

Index-Contributors

Index-Recipes

Vegetables & Side Dishes

Main Dishes

Beef/Pork/Lamb

Main Dishes

Chicken

Light &
Delicious

California Cookbook Company
1907 Skycrest Drive
Fullerton, CA 92631

Please send me _____ copy(ies) of *Light & Delicious* at **$9.95**ea (includes tax and postage).
Make checks payable to *California Cookbook Company.*
Enclosed is my check for _____ book(s) at $9.95 each $_____.

Name _____

Street _____

City _____ State _____ Zip _____

Light &
Delicious

California Cookbook Company
1907 Skycrest Drive
Fullerton, CA 92631

Please send me _____ copy(ies) of *Light & Delicious* at **$9.95**ea (includes tax and postage).
Make checks payable to *California Cookbook Company.*
Enclosed is my check for _____ book(s) at $9.95 each $_____.

Name _____

Street _____

City _____ State _____ Zip _____

Light &
Delicious

California Cookbook Company
1907 Skycrest Drive
Fullerton, CA 92631

Please send me _____ copy(ies) of *Light & Delicious* at **$9.95**ea (includes tax and postage).
Make checks payable to *California Cookbook Company.*
Enclosed is my check for _____ book(s) at $9.95 each $_____.

Name _____

Street _____

City _____ State _____ Zip _____